PRAISE FOR *BUILDING CHAM*

MW01070394

Carol Miller's book *Building Champions* is absolutely the best group curriculum... boys out there. The activities, themes, handouts, and materials are easily laid out for school counselors to follow and implement in their school counseling programs. Additionally, the curriculum is aligned with the ASCA Mindsets and Behaviors, which is an extra bonus! I would highly recommend *Building Champions* to every school counselor.

> — Malti Tuttle, PhD
> School Counselor, Marietta, Georgia

Who better than a school counselor to design a curriculum for champions? Carol Miller has focused on how boys can improve their academic, social/emotional, and career goals to become champions. I love how she has used a variety of learning styles to focus on each student's strength. See for yourself how this resource can improve your program.

> — Lisa Koenecke, MS, MCC
> Middle School Counselor, River Bluff, Wisconsin
> Past President, Wisconsin School Counselor Association

This is the book you've been waiting for. It is a comprehensive and effective program, and it is filled with everything you need to run a group for middle school boys. It is also easily adaptable for high school and upper elementary students. The activities are appealing, straightforward, easily implemented, and fill the requirements for any developmental guidance program. This should be in any good counselor's library.

> — Gaye Dunn, MS
> Middle School Counselor, East Moline, Illinois

As a middle school counselor, I often see boys as an underserved population in the school environment. In *Building Champions,* Carol Miller provides a much-needed and hard-to-find resource that helps boys develop self-leadership skills while also addressing the external arenas of relationships, leadership, teamwork, and sportsmanship. This small-group curriculum fills an obvious gap in the growth of boys, providing a path to self-development and maturity. Kudos to Carol Miller for creating a user-friendly resource benefiting boys in their development.

> — Jan Desmarais-Morse, MEd
> Middle School Counselor and Counselor Educator,
> Goshen, Indiana

Carol Miller truly understands the nature of boys! Being a mother of three boys and a school counselor to hundreds more, I appreciate the hands-on activities and analogies that she uses throughout *Building Champions.*

> — Mindy Willard, MA
> High School Counselor, Franklin, Wisconsin
> 2013 American School Counselor of the Year

BUILDING Champions

A SMALL-GROUP COUNSELING CURRICULUM FOR BOYS

CAROL MILLER

RESEARCH PRESS
PUBLISHERS

2612 North Mattis Avenue, Champaign, Illinois 61822
800.519.2707 / researchpress.com

RESEARCH PRESS
PUBLISHERS

Copyright © 2016 by Carol Miller

5 4 3 2 1   16 17 18 19 20

All rights reserved. Printed in the United States of America.

In this book, items including the Research Press credit line may be reproduced with proper credit to the source for noncommercial educational or clinical use by the original purchaser only, not to extend to reproduction by other parties. Excerpts may be printed in connection with published reviews in periodicals without express permission. No other part of this book may be reproduced by any means, or stored in a database or retrieval system, without the written permission of the publisher.

Table on page 6 adapted by permission from *Mindsets and Behaviors for Student Success: K–12 College- and Career-readiness Standards for Every Student,* © 2014 by the American School Counselor Association.

Building Champions Small-Group Action Plan (in Appendix B) adapted by permission from *The ASCA National Model: A Framework for School Counseling Programs* (3rd ed.), © 2012 by the American School Counselor Association.

Copies of this book may be ordered from Research Press at the address given on the title page.

Composition by Jeff Helgesen
Cover design by McKenzie Wagner, Inc.
Printed by Edwards Brothers Malloy.

ISBN 978-0-87822-699-3
Library of Congress Control Number 2016933071

CONTENTS

ACKNOWLEDGMENTS

To my family—Mark, Hayden, Cullen, and Charlie: I love you all and thank you for all your support. Thank you for supporting me when I am up all night working on the computer. To my dad, whom I will never forget; you will always be a part of me. You are all, and always will be, champions.

To my friends Jan, Sandy, and Alyssa, for being a sounding board for my ideas.

To Julia, for giving me courage to pursue a dream.

ABOUT THE BUILDING CHAMPIONS PROGRAM

WHY HAVE A BOYS' GROUP?

Let's face it—those of us who have boys know that they can be a handful. Young boys are full of life, full of energy, and full of hope. It's not surprising to hear parents talk about the difference between raising boys and girls. Boys are rougher, messier, and always into something. But it can be hard to grow up male in today's society. Many boys growing up today lack the opportunities and resources to establish male bonding and identity groups. Many boys today also have few male role models because most schoolteachers are female and the majority of single-parent households are run by women. In addition, African American students and those from lower economic backgrounds may encounter even fewer healthy alternatives for defining their male identity than do their white and wealthier counterparts (Mid-Atlantic Equity Consortium, 2010).

In schools, boys are four to five times more likely than girls to be diagnosed with Attention Deficit/Hyperactivity Disorder (Thompson, n.d.), and boys are more likely to disrupt class than girls. Boys who disrupt class and do not feel academically engaged are also more likely to do poorly in middle school (Downey & Vogt Yuan, 2005). For students who are held back a grade level, middle school boys are retained twice as often as their female counterparts (U. S. Department of Education, 2012). When it comes to grades and homework, girls outperform boys in elementary, secondary, high school, college, and even graduate school, and women outnumber men in higher education, with 56 percent of bachelor's degrees and 55 percent of graduate degrees going to women (Thompson, n.d.).

A boys' empowerment group can help members grow and support one another, avoid risky behavior like gang involvement, and encourage boys to make healthy choices that can lead to positive growth (Hall & Charmaraman, 2011). Boys who need support in choosing positive and healthy pathways can benefit from an intervention that gives them space and time to share information, to work and play cooperatively, and to grow healthy identities. While inclusive grouping is an important part of building community in a youth development program, common-interest groups such as girls' or boys' empowerment groups can help members grow and provide mutual support (Mid-Atlantic Equity Consortium, 2010).

PROGRAM OVERVIEW

The Building Champions program is a small-group counseling program designed to help upper elementary through middle school boys build trust, respect, and peer connections while reducing classroom conflicts, discipline issues, and anxiety. Building Champions uses many active learning activities that will help maintain students' interest and allow them to practice targeted skills while learning. Active learning such as that promoted in this program has been found to help students grasp concepts more quickly, engage with the material being presented, and be active participants in the learning process (Jackson, 1993).

LESSON FORMAT

This group curriculum uses an experiential learning model. In each lesson, students are asked to complete an active learning activity and then are led through a series of questions that ask the students to reflect on each stage of their learning:

- *What?* What happened? What were the results?
- *So what?* What do the results means?
- *Now what?* Where do we go from here?

Each lesson follows a set procedure:

- Warm-up: 5 minutes
- Activity: 20–25 minutes
- Discussion: 5–10 minutes
- Evaluation: 5 minutes

Through this format, students quickly grasp concepts and easily identify how the activity connects to future learning and experiences.

LESSON SCHEDULING

Ideally, this group program should meet weekly over the course of eight weeks. Each lesson is designed to take place during a 35- to 45-minute class period. You can choose to meet with your group during lunch, an elective or encore class, or an advisor/advisee period. You may use a rotating class schedule or conduct lessons after school. You should choose a schedule that will work best within your school or program setting. Several factors that you should take into consideration when scheduling your groups include the needs and preferences of classroom teachers, school activities that students may miss (including lunch and recess), and the ability to minimize interruptions to avoid losing the attention and focus of the group.

GROUP COMPOSITION AND OTHER REQUIREMENTS

For upper elementary and middle school students, the optimal group size is between 6 and 8 students. The program is adaptable for secondary-level students. In that case, groups may be increased to 12 students. More than that number can decrease the effectiveness of the group. Groups may include boys who are friends but ideally should not include only members of the same friend grouping. A mixture of several friend groupings would be best. In addition, it may be helpful to have at least one boy who is a positive role model among his classmates.

The program's active learning activities require space for the boys to move around, so a setting permitting this will be required. A photocopier or printer is needed for producing various handouts; other necessary materials include a whiteboard or poster board, writing utensils, and basic art supplies. Other materials, specified in each lesson, are generally available in the classroom.

LESSON OPTIONS

Each Building Champions lesson is meant to build upon the prior one, and for Lessons 2 through 7, three different lesson options are provided. The group leader is encouraged to preview and read over all the lesson choices and make a decision based on the group's needs. Options typically include a low-level activity and a more active, higher energy activity to choose from. Discussion questions that follow the lesson allow the boys to further converse and learn from the activity. Each group culminates with boys' filling out an "Exit Slip" that will help you, as a leader, assess whether the students are walking away with an understanding of the objectives of the lesson. (Exit Slips are provided in Appendix A.)

GENERAL GUIDELINES FOR GROUP LEADERS

You don't need to be an expert to lead a group. You just have to be willing to start and have fun. Be optimistic, energetic, and patient. It might take a session or two for the boys to bond, get comfortable with one another, and work together. Being positive yourself will have a positive effect on the boys and will inspire them to take your lead. Monitor group interaction to ensure that all boys are participating. Encourage participation, especially by those who are shy or hesitant to share. However, always allow students to have the option of a "pass" if they are uncomfortable sharing.

Always be prepared for boys to share information that may be too personal, inappropriate, or off topic. This is particularly the case with younger students. If a boy shares too much, thank him for his contribution and let him know that group time is limited but that you would love to talk with him more about his disclosure during a time after group. With older boys, remind them of the group rules and ask the boy who is sharing if he is comfortable sharing with the other group members.

Understand the limits of confidentiality and take appropriate action if a member engages in behavior that presents a clear and imminent danger to himself or others or discloses physical or sexual abuse. Establishing confidentiality in the group will allow the boys to feel they have a safe place to share their concerns, ask questions, and let their guard down. It is through this ability to share freely that the best results occur. If a situation occurs where you, as the leader, feel that you must disclose confidential information, let the member know ahead of time that you plan to do it and what you plan to say.

If conflict arises within the group, use the group process to identify the problem and resolve the issue. Acknowledge the boys' feelings and offer your guidance. Discuss with the group how they feel about the conflict and make sure each boy feels heard.

Use open-ended questioning to encourage student dialogue. Ask, "Why," "How," and "What" rather than asking questions that look for a simple yes or no response. Specific phrases that can encourage discussion include these:

- "Can you tell us more about…"
- "Help us understand…"
- "Explain to us…"
- "Can you share an example of…"

Most important, be ready to get moving, get talking, and have fun!

ASCA MINDSETS AND BEHAVIORS

The ASCA Mindsets and Behaviors for Student Success (American School Counselor Association, 2014) provide a framework for school counseling programs, and the Building Champions program has been developed to meet the student competencies the model identifies. The table on the following page lists ASCA mindsets and behaviors that are met by the Building Champions program. The Building Champions Small-Group Action Plan, adapted from ASCA materials (American School Counselor Association, 2012) and included in Appendix B, will help you in your endeavors in developing a comprehensive school curriculum plan and Recognized ASCA Model Program.

PROGRAM ORGANIZATION AND EVALUATION

Various forms to help you start your Building Champions group and keep track of your group's progress are included in the last two appendixes of this book. Appendix B provides program organization and progress tracking forms. The forms in Appendix C will be useful in collecting data, analyzing it, and reporting it back to stakeholders—essential steps in any counseling intervention. The data collected on these forms can not only identify areas of concern but also document the knowledge gained and changes in attitudes and beliefs of the boys involved. Included is a parent letter used to obtain permission for group counseling and evaluation and a parent follow-up evaluation form, which should be sent home to notify parents that the group has ended and to check in to see if parents have noticed an improvement in behavior and attitude at home. The group member follow-up survey also provided should be given to the group about four weeks after the group has ended. The information you collect on these and other forms will help you to evaluate the group's effectiveness and share your findings with other interested parties.

ASCA Mindsets and Behaviors for Student Success Addressed by the Building Champions Program

Category 1: Mindset Standards

School counselors encourage the following mindsets for all students:

- Belief in development of whole self, including a healthy balance of mental, social/emotional, and physical well-being (MS–1)
- Self-confidence in ability to succeed (MS–2)
- Sense of belonging in the school environment (MS–3)
- Belief in using abilities to their fullest to achieve high-quality results and outcomes (MS–4)
- Positive attitude toward work and learning (MS–5)

Category 2: Behavior Standards

Students will demonstrate the following standards through classroom lessons, activities and/or individual/small-group counseling.

Learning Strategies

- Demonstrate critical-thinking skills to make informed decisions (LS–1)
- Gather evidence and consider multiple perspectives to make informed decisions (LS–9)

Self-Management Skills

- Demonstrate ability to assume responsibility (SM–1)
- Demonstrate self-discipline and self-control (SM–2)
- Demonstrate ability to delay immediate gratification for long-term rewards (SM–4)
- Demonstrate effective coping skills when faced with a problem (SM–7)
- Demonstrate personal safety skills (SM–9)
- Demonstrate ability to manage transitions and ability to adapt to changing situations and responsibilities (SM–10)

Social Skills

- Use effective oral and written communication skills and listening skills (SS–1)
- Create positive and supportive relationships with other students (SS–2)
- Create relationships with adults that support success (SS–3)
- Demonstrate empathy (SS–4)
- Demonstrate ethical decision making and social responsibility (SS–5)
- Use effective collaboration and cooperation skills (SS–6)
- Use leadership and teamwork skills to work effectively in diverse teams (SS–7)
- Demonstrate advocacy skills and ability to assert self, when necessary (SS–8)
- Demonstrate social maturity and behaviors appropriate to the situation and environment (SS–9)

Introduction to Building Champions

What Is a Champion?

LEARNING OBJECTIVES

- Boys will understand the purpose of the group and the reasons they are participating.

- Boys will understand the group rules and expectations.

- Boys will define *champion* and describe the importance of being a champion.

- Boys will be introduced to words of empowerment.

KEY CONCEPT

A champion is more than someone who wins a sporting contest or event. A champion exhibits exemplary personal values and character traits. A champion also overcomes obstacles and is someone who meets his own personal goals. A champion is someone who learns lessons from losses and strives to become the best version of himself.

MATERIALS

- In This Team poster (1.1), reproduced and hung in the classroom
- A copy for each boy:

  Team Contract (1.2)

  A Champion Is… (1.3)

  My Self-Portrait (1.4)

  Lesson 1 Exit Slip (from Appendix A)

  Building Champions Pretest/Posttest (from Appendix B)
- Writing utensils
- Markers, paint, and other craft materials for coloring

PROCEDURE

Warm-up

Have each boy complete the following sentences:

- I would define a champion as someone who…

- One champion I know is…and this person is a champion because…

Activity

1. Explain that the purpose of the group is to help boys become more confident, cope with stressors at school, build better friendships, become better leaders, and have fun.

2. Go over the In This Team poster. Explain the group rules and allow boys to add one or two more. Explain the importance of confidentiality.

3. Hand each boy a Team Contract. Ask boys to sign the contract if they are willing to abide by the group's rules.

4. Have boys compete the Building Champions Pretest/Posttest.

5. Hand each boy an A Champion Is…worksheet. Break the group into partners. Ask the boys to brainstorm the characteristics they believe makes someone a champion as well as those that prevent someone from being his best.

6. Hand each boy a My Self-Portrait worksheet and distribute the art supplies. Ask the boys to draw themselves as a champion, including the positive characteristics that they believe would make them a champion.

Discussion

Ask the group the following questions:

- How do you feel about the rules we established today? Do you think you will be able to honor the rules we have established?

- Why is it important to define a champion as someone with good character rather than as someone who wins a contest?

- Why is it important for you to try your best?

- What is the difference between a winner and a champion?

- If a person believes himself to be a champion, does he then become a winner at life?

- Do you think that you will enjoy coming to group?

Evaluation

STUDENT

- Give each student a Lesson 1 Exit Slip to fill out, share, and hand in before leaving.

- Did the students agree to the rules that were established?

- Did each boy actively participate in the activities?

In This Team

1. Champions do their best.

2. Champions do not interrupt.

3. Champions are respectful.

4. Champions are kind.

_____

_____

From *Building Champions: A Small-Group Counseling Curriculum for Boys,* by C. Miller,
© 2016, Champaign, IL: Research Press (800-519-2707, www.researchpress.com).

Team Contract

As a Building Champions team member, I agree to follow all group rules:

- I understand and respect confidentiality. What we talk about in team stays in team.

- I will do my best. I will contribute to activities and conversations and have a positive attitude. I may "pass" on an activity if I am not comfortable sharing my experiences.

- I will not interrupt. One person speaks at a time, and everyone has the right to be heard. I will also listen to others, even though I may disagree with them.

- I will be respectful. Everyone has an opportunity to participate and share. I will use only respectful words and behaviors.

- I will be kind. I will encourage other team members to do their best.

_____

Team member's signature

_____

Leader's signature

_____

Date

From *Building Champions: A Small-Group Counseling Curriculum for Boys,* by C. Miller, © 2016, Champaign, IL: Research Press (800-519-2707, www.researchpress.com).

A Champion Is...

Name_____ Date_____

Work together to determine the qualities of someone who is a champion versus the qualities of someone who is not a champion.

A Champion Is	A Champion Is Not

From *Building Champions: A Small-Group Counseling Curriculum for Boys,* by C. Miller, © 2016, Champaign, IL: Research Press (800-519-2707, www.researchpress.com).

My Self-Portrait

Name _____ Date _____

In the frame below, draw yourself as a champion. Be sure to include all the qualities you believe make you a champion.

From *Building Champions: A Small-Group Counseling Curriculum for Boys,* by C. Miller,
© 2016, Champaign, IL: Research Press (800-519-2707, www.researchpress.com).

Breaking a Sweat
(Goal Setting)

Goal Setting

LEARNING OBJECTIVES

- Each boy will understand why it is important to set personal goals.
- Boys will be able to define a SMART goal.
- Boys will write SMART goals.
- Boys will create their own SMART goal.

KEY CONCEPT

Goal setting is an important concept for creating change that results in success. SMART goals help ensure that the goal-setting process results in success. Setting SMART goals hold us accountable for their attainment and makes goals that seem impossible achievable.

MATERIALS

- Breaking a Sweat Questions (2.1), copied and cut apart and placed in a bowl or jar
- SMART Goals poster (2.2), reproduced and hung in the classroom
- A copy for each boy:

    Goal Setting (2.3)

    Writing SMART Goals (2.4)

    My SMART Plan for Success (2.5)

    Lesson 2 Exit Slip (from Appendix A)

- Writing utensils

PROCEDURE

Warm-up

Have the boys draw Breaking a Sweat Questions and answer them. You may have the boys either answer their own question or ask the person on their right. To add interest, questions may also be written on craft sticks.

Activity

1. Direct students' attention to the SMART Goals poster and give each student a Goal Setting handout. Discuss and share examples of SMART goals.

2. Have students complete the Writing SMART Goals worksheet and go over as a group.

3. Have students complete their own SMART goal on the My SMART Plan for Success worksheet.

Discussion

Ask the boys the following questions:

- Do you think you will be more likely to achieve your goal because it is a SMART goal?

- Why is it important to put time limits on goals?

- Why does a goal need to be relevant?

- Why do you need to evaluate your goals?

- Do you think people make goals that are too big and then give up on them?

- How will you feel if you meet your goal?

Evaluation

STUDENT

- Give each student a Lesson 2 Exit Slip to fill out, share, and hand in before leaving.

LEADER

- Was each boy able to write his own SMART goal?

- Did each boy understand the importance of setting goals?

Accountability

LEARNING OBJECTIVES

- Boys will be able to define *accountability*.
- Boys will understand how their actions affect others.
- Boys will learn the importance of team roles within a group.

KEY CONCEPT

Accountability is taking account of one's own actions. Our actions may have an impact on more than just ourselves. In school, at home, and at work, our actions can affect other people. When we understand the cause and effect relationship associated with our actions, then we can begin to make better choices for our behavior.

MATERIALS

- Breaking a Sweat Questions (2.1), copied, cut apart, and placed in bowl or jar
- A copy for each boy:

  Team Build Instructions (2.6)

  Lesson 2 Exit Slip (from Appendix A)
- For each team of four: Scissors, two small balls of clay, two straws, hole punch
- Whistle
- Writing utensils

PREPARATION

Fill two zippered plastic bags (or small trays or boxes) for each team with the Team Build Parts (2.7) and other materials needed for the team to complete the Sailboat and Palm Tree builds. Include a copy of the appropriate Team Build Materials Checklist (2.8) for each item.

PROCEDURE

Warm-up

Have the boys draw Breaking a Sweat Questions and answer them. You may have the boys either answer their own question or ask the person on their right. To add interest, questions may also be written on craft sticks.

Activity

1. Break the boys up into groups of four. Each group of four will form an "assembly line" by sitting side by side next to each other.

2. Explain to students that they must work together with their teammates as part of an assembly line and, as quickly as possible, try to create a sailboat from the materials they are given.

3. Give a zippered bag to the student sitting at the left end of each assembly line and blow a whistle to start the game.

4. The first member, while remaining seated, must hand out copies of the Team Build Instructions for the sailboat to his teammates. He should also complete the first step of the sailboat project. When he is finished building his section of the sailboat, he should pass his portion of the project down the assembly line. Teammates 2, 3, and 4 should follow their directions and continue assembling the sailboat, each passing their section of the boat down to the next teammate assembler. The first team to assemble the sailboat is the winner.

5. Discuss with the boys their perceptions of the activity. Ask: "What would help your group to be more efficient in putting together your sailboat?"

6. Make sure teammates are in their lines and proceed with building the palm tree according to the instructions in the Team Build Instructions.

7. Discuss with the boys the definition of *accountability*. (Define it as taking responsibility for one's own actions.)

Discussion

Ask the boys the following questions:

- What happened in this activity?

- What does this activity have to do with accountability?

- Why did each teammate need to be accountable?

- Did you have a different level of accountability based on your place in line?

- Did the first or last teammate need to be more accountable? Why?

- How can you relate this activity to school?

- How can you relate this activity to life outside of school?

- What did you learn from this activity?

Evaluation

STUDENT

- Give each student a Lesson 2 Exit Slip to fill out, share, and hand in before leaving.

LEADER

- Did each boy actively participate in the team builds?

- Were the boys able to relate this activity to the classroom and life outside the classroom?

OPTION 3

Being Disciplined

LEARNING OBJECTIVES

- Boys will understand the difference between discipline and self-discipline.

- Boys will practice self-discipline.

- Boys will recognize ways to practice self-control while under pressure.

KEY CONCEPT

Discipline is behaving according to rules. *Self-discipline* is being able to restrain one's actions (for example, controlling one's emotions). While sometimes we enter situations where we must exercise discipline, we must also be able to be self-disciplined. Recess, classroom projects, and sporting events are all examples of areas where we have certain rules to follow (discipline) but we must also keep our cool (self-discipline), even when these rules are sometimes broken or disregarded by others.

MATERIALS

- Breaking a Sweat Questions (2.1), copied, cut apart, and placed in a bowl or jar

- Two individually wrapped candies per student (with one placed at each boy's desk before he enters the room)

- A copy for each boy:

  Under Control (2.9)

  Lesson 2 Exit Slip (from Appendix A)

- Writing utensils

PROCEDURE

Warm-up

1. As soon as the students arrive, ask them to unwrap their candies. Tell them that they have a choice: They may eat the candy immediately, or they may leave it on their desks until the end of the lesson, in which case they will receive a second piece of candy.

2. Have the boys draw Breaking a Sweat Questions and answer them. You may have the boys either answer their own question or ask the person on their right. To add interest, questions may also be written on craft sticks.

Activity

1. Discuss the terms *discipline* and *self-discipline* with the boys. Brainstorm with them:

   ▪ Define *discipline.*

   ▪ Can you give an example of why discipline is important?

   ▪ Define *self-discipline.*

   ▪ What are some examples of being self-disciplined?

2. Distribute the Under Control worksheets to the boys. Allow boys time to complete their worksheets, then discuss as a group.

3. When you are done going over the worksheet, give the boys who have not eaten their candy a second piece and tell them it's now okay to eat both pieces.

Discussion

Ask the boys the following questions:

▪ What did you notice during this activity?

▪ Was the candy a distraction?

▪ Why is discipline important?

▪ Why is self-discipline important?

▪ What situations in life call for you to have self-discipline?

▪ How can you practice self-discipline if you feel like you are losing control?

▪ What are some strategies you can use to maintain self-discipline?

▪ What did the candy experiment help you understand about self-discipline?

Evaluation

STUDENT

▪ Give each student a Lesson 2 Exit Slip to fill out, share, and hand in before leaving.

- Did each boy actively participate in the activities?

- Were the boys able to practice self-discipline by not eating the candy?

Breaking a Sweat Questions

What is your favorite thing to do on a Saturday?	What is one thing you are afraid of?
Would you rather play a board game or a card game? Why?	What is your favorite movie?
What is your favorite subject?	What do you like to do in your free time?
Whom do you live with?	If you could choose a month for your birthday, which month would you choose? Why?
What is a hobby you enjoy?	What are three things you enjoy doing?
What is something you enjoy doing by yourself?	What is your favorite dessert?
What are three traits that best describe you?	What do you do on the weekend?
How would your teachers describe you?	If you could paint your bedroom, what color would it be?
How would your family describe you?	Would you rather play in the sand or the snow? Why?
What is something you would like to do when you're older?	What is your favorite food?
What is your favorite color?	Do you prefer milk or juice?

From *Building Champions: A Small-Group Counseling Curriculum for Boys,* by C. Miller, © 2016, Champaign, IL: Research Press (800-519-2707, www.researchpress.com).

SMART Goals

S   Specific—What exactly will you do?

M   Measurable—How will you know you will meet your goal?

A   Achievable—Can you actually do it?

R   Relative—How much does it mean to you?

T   Timely—When will you accomplish your goal?

From *Building Champions: A Small-Group Counseling Curriculum for Boys,* by C. Miller,
© 2016, Champaign, IL: Research Press (800-519-2707, www.researchpress.com).

Goal Setting

Name _____ Date _____

Let's think about this goal: "I want to get good grades."

Do you have a clear understanding when this will happen? What does a good grade mean (is it an A, a B, or a C)? Does this statement tell you how you will accomplish this goal? Does it say why it is important?

We could also say: "I am going to travel across the country."

This may happen, but having a SMART goal is like saying I am going from New York to California by car, I have a map, and I know my travel route, how long it will take me, and how much it will cost. In other words, I have a plan.

Let's go back to our first goal: "I want to get good grades." Let's turn it into a SMART goal.

Specific—means exact. Specific says I want to get an 85 for my third marking period social studies grade.

Measurable—means you are able to tell if you are meeting your goals or not. Checking weekly for a grade update will help to let you know if you are meeting the goal of 85 in social studies class.

Achievable—means (with some work) you can reach your goal. If you set your goal too high, you may not be able to reach it. Saying you want an 85 in a class may be realistic for some, but for others it may not be achievable.

Relevant—tells why this goal is important to you. For example: "If I get an 85 in social studies I will get to go to camp this summer."

Timely—Tells when you will reach this goal. For example, you could say you will reach this goal in 10 weeks. Just be sure you give yourself enough time to reach your goal. Likewise, don't leave so much time that you forget about it.

From *Building Champions: A Small-Group Counseling Curriculum for Boys,* by C. Miller, © 2016, Champaign, IL: Research Press (800-519-2707, www.researchpress.com).

Writing SMART Goals

Name _____ Date _____

Why do we need goals?

_____

_____

Why do goals need to be:

Specific _____

Measurable _____

Achievable _____

Relevant _____

Timely _____

Review

Goal: "I want to get good grades."

> Do you have a clear understanding when this will happen? What does a good grade mean (is it an A, a B, or a C)? Does this statement tell you how you will accomplish this goal? Does it say why it is important?

SMART goal: "In 10 weeks I want to get an 85 in social studies. I will stay after to work with the teacher, study for tests, do my homework, and ask questions when I do not understand. This goal is important to me because my parents told me they will send me to summer camp if I can get an 85 on my next report card. I will check with my teacher each week to see how I am progressing toward my goal."

From *Building Champions: A Small-Group Counseling Curriculum for Boys,* by C. Miller,
© 2016, Champaign, IL: Research Press (800-519-2707, www.researchpress.com).

(Handout 2.4, continued)

Rewrite the following goals to make them SMART goals.

1. I want to get good grades.

   _____

   _____

2. I will not get in trouble at school.

   _____

   _____

3. I will not spend so much time playing video games.

   _____

   _____

4. I want to join a club or sport.

   _____

   _____

My SMART Plan for Success

Name _____ Date _____

S   **Specific**—What exactly will you do?

M   **Measurable**—How will you know you will meet your goal?

A   **Achievable**—Can you actually do it?

R   **Relevant**—How much does it mean to you?

T   **Timely**—When will you accomplish your goal?

1. What is my **Specific** goal? What do I want to improve?

    What are the actions I plan to take to reach this goal?

    _____

    _____

    _____

2. How will I show I have **Measurable** success in reaching my goal?

From *Building Champions: A Small-Group Counseling Curriculum for Boys,* by C. Miller,
© 2016, Champaign, IL: Research Press (800-519-2707, www.researchpress.com).

3. Who can help make my goal **Achievable?**

Who or what can prevent me from reaching my goal?

_____

_____

_____

4. Why is my goal important to me and **Relevant?**

5. When will I complete my goal **(Timely)?**

Team Build Instructions

Team Build: Sailboat

Teammate 1: Pass out instructions to your teammates. Cut a triangle out of the paper rectangle for the sail.

Teammate 2: Punch three holes into the sail and roll the clay into a ball.

Teammate 3: Insert the straw through the holes in the sail. Attach the clay to the bottom of the straw.

Teammate 4: Cut the boat bottom and attach the clay at the bottom of the sail to the boat. Announce when you are done.

Team Build: Palm Tree

Teammate 1: Pass out instructions to your teammates. Cut four strips of paper for the palm fronds.

Teammate 2: Split the clay into two balls. Roll one ball into a log and form a ring around the top of the straw (this is to hold the palm fronds).

Teammate 3: Punch a hole on one side of each palm frond. Put the straw through the holes and form the palm tree. You may need to fix the clay so the palm leaves stay at the top of the tree.

Teammate 4: Cut out the paper circle. This will be the ground. Attach the tree to the ground using the clay ball. Announce when you are done.

From *Building Champions: A Small-Group Counseling Curriculum for Boys,* by C. Miller, © 2016, Champaign, IL: Research Press (800-519-2707, www.researchpress.com).

Team Build Parts

SAILBOAT

Sail

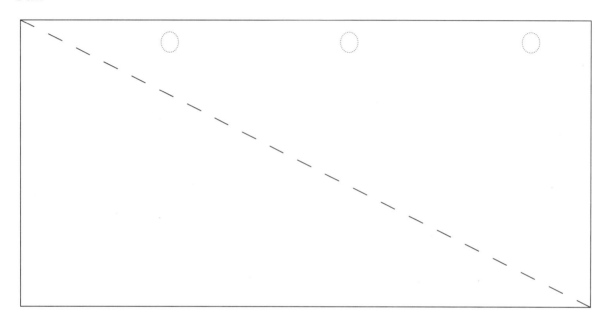

Boat bottom

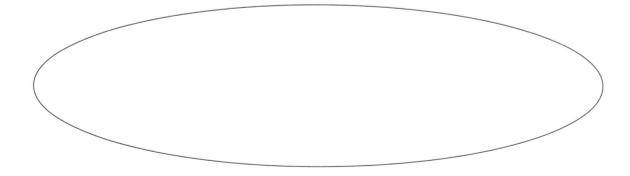

From *Building Champions: A Small-Group Counseling Curriculum for Boys,* by C. Miller,
© 2016, Champaign, IL: Research Press (800-519-2707, www.researchpress.com).

(Handout 2.7, continued)

PALM TREE

Palm fronds

Ground

Team Build Materials Checklists

Team Build:
Sailboat Building Supplies

- ☐ Paper rectangle for sail
- ☐ Boat bottom
- ☐ Pair of scissors
- ☐ Straw
- ☐ Hole punch
- ☐ Ball of clay

Team Build:
Sailboat Building Supplies

- ☐ Paper rectangle for sail
- ☐ Boat bottom
- ☐ Pair of scissors
- ☐ Straw
- ☐ Hole punch
- ☐ Ball of clay

Team Build:
Palm Tree Building Supplies

- ☐ Paper palm fronds
- ☐ Ground
- ☐ Pair of scissors
- ☐ Straw
- ☐ Hole punch
- ☐ Ball of clay

Team Build:
Palm Tree Building Supplies

- ☐ Paper palm fronds
- ☐ Ground
- ☐ Pair of scissors
- ☐ Straw
- ☐ Hole punch
- ☐ Ball of clay

From *Building Champions: A Small-Group Counseling Curriculum for Boys,* by C. Miller, © 2016, Champaign, IL: Research Press (800-519-2707, www.researchpress.com).

Under Control

Name _____ Date _____

Discipline is different from being self-disciplined.

To understand the difference, think of a basketball game:

> **Discipline** means to behave or act according to rules. If we were at a basketball game, players must follow a set of rules, or they would be removed from play. Players show discipline by following the rules of fair play.

> **Self-disciplined** means being able to restrain oneself or one's actions, such as by controlling one's emotions. If a basketball player was hit or blocked by a member of the opposing team, he could get angry. Keeping his anger to himself and not letting others see it shows his self-discipline.

> *Now it's your turn. How do you show that you have discipline and self-discipline:*

1. I show I have discipline by _____

   _____

   _____

   _____

2. I show I have self-discipline by _____

   _____

   _____

   _____

From *Building Champions: A Small-Group Counseling Curriculum for Boys,* by C. Miller,
© 2016, Champaign, IL: Research Press (800-519-2707, www.researchpress.com).

Describe the difference between discipline (the rules) and how you could exercise self-discipline in each of the following situations.

Situation	Discipline	Self-Discipline
1. You hate homework. Your dad said you have to finish your homework before playing video games.		
2. The boy behind you in class was talking, but you got in trouble because the teacher thought it was you.		
3. You want to be on the varsity track team, so you get up extra early every morning to run.		
4. You are working on a group project, and one of your group members is ignoring every suggestion you give.		

In the Huddle
(Integrity and Respect)

Integrity

LEARNING OBJECTIVES

- Each boy will be able to define *integrity*.

- Boys will understand the importance of having integrity.

- Boys will reflect on how they wish to be thought of by others.

KEY CONCEPT

Integrity can be defined as doing the right thing even when no one is watching. Integrity is a characteristic that others may judge us by. Having integrity allows people to trust us. Having integrity means you are honest to others as well as yourself.

MATERIALS

- Labels Directions for Group Leaders (3.1)

- Labels Cards (3.2), photocopied and cut apart

- A copy for each boy:

  How Do I Want to Be Remembered? (3.3)

  Remember Me (3.4)

  Integrity (3.5)

  Lesson 3 Exit Slip (from Appendix A)

- Highlighters

- Tape

- Small dish of lemon juice

- Cotton swabs or small paintbrushes

- Towel or ironing board and iron

PROCEDURE

Warm-up

Have the boys play the Labels game according to the instructions on the Labels Directions for Group Leaders.

Activity

1. Distribute a How Do I Want to Be Remembered? worksheet to each student. Allow the boys time to read the worksheet and circle the negative character trait words. Have them highlight, on the Remember Me worksheet, the 10 words that they would like others to use to describe them.

2. Have the boys share their 10 positive character traits with the group. Ask the boys to raise a hand if someone calls out a word they also have highlighted.

3. Ask the boys: "Which word or words were the most common among you?"

4. After all the boys have shared, discuss what *integrity* means. Define integrity as doing the right thing even when no one is watching. Discuss how the words the boys picked to describe themselves describe their integrity. Ask the boys:

   ▪ What does "doing the right thing even when no one is watching" mean?

   ▪ What are some examples that you can share of what this means?

5. Hand out the Integrity worksheets and cotton swabs to each boy. Set the lemon juice (invisible ink) in the middle of the table. Have the boys write with their "invisible ink" what integrity means to them.

6. Collect the worksheets from the boys. Place them facedown on an ironing board or towel on a table. Reveal their definitions of integrity by ironing the back of the worksheets.

Discussion

Ask the boys:

▪ What happened in this activity?

▪ How is what we wrote on our papers with invisible ink like integrity?

▪ Why is it important for us to have others think positively of us?

▪ When other people think of you as a person with integrity, how do you feel?

▪ What is your definition of *integrity?*

▪ Do champions value integrity?

▪ How can we apply what we learned to school and life outside of school?

Evaluation

- Give each student a Lesson 3 Exit Slip to fill out, share, and hand in before leaving.

- Did the boys actively participate in the activities?

- Did each boy understand the importance of integrity?

Respect

LEARNING OBJECTIVES

- Each boy will generate examples of what respect is and is not.
- Boys will see respect as a valued trait.
- Boys will practice kindness.

KEY CONCEPT

Respect is how you treat someone and how you feel about him or her. Respect is also the ability to accept others' opinions even if they differ from your own. We show respect for others by showing we care about their feelings and well-being.

MATERIALS

- Copy of the Labels Directions for Group Leaders (3.1)
- Labels Cards, photocopied and cut apart (3.2)
- Whiteboard or poster board and markers
- A cereal box for each group of four boys
- Construction paper (enough to cover and decorate each cereal box)
- Glue and tape
- Markers, crayons, and other craft supplies for decorating
- Writing utensils
- A copy of the Lesson 3 Exit Slip for each boy (from Appendix A)

PROCEDURE

Warm-up

Have the boys play the Labels game according to the instructions on the Labels Directions for Group Leaders.

Activity

1. Begin a discussion with the boys about respect. Have them come up with a definition of *respect* and write it on a whiteboard or poster board.

2. Write "Respect Is" on the left side of the board and "Respect Is Not" on the right side of the board. Ask the boys to provide examples of each. For example:

   - Respect Is: Listening to others when they are talking, helping other people, being kind, not taking things that belong to other people, using good manners

   - Respect Is Not: Not listening to other people, talking when the teacher is talking, not helping others, calling people names, arguing with other people

3. After the boys have given examples, break the boys into groups of four. Give each group a cereal box and materials to decorate their box. Instruct the boys that they are to create a product that will give the consumer "respect" when used. Give the boys 15 minutes to develop their product, decorate their box, and create a commercial to sell their product.

4. After 15 minutes have passed, have all the groups come together and present their commercials to the class. Allow students to vote at the end for the best product and commercial.

Discussion

Ask the boys:

- Tell me what we did in this activity.

- What did you need to do as a group to get this project done?

- Did the time constraints help or hurt your group and why?

- Did everyone in your group feel respected?

- What if we could buy respect from a box?

- What are ways we show respect?

- How do others show respect to you?

- Why is respect important?

- What did this activity teach you about respect?

Evaluation

- Give each student a Lesson 3 Exit Slip to fill out, share, and hand in before leaving.

- Was each boy able to work as part of a team?

- Was each team able to accomplish the assignment?

Fair Play

LEARNING OBJECTIVES

- Each boy will understand what fair play means.

- Boys will understand why fair play is important.

KEY CONCEPT

Fair play is the ability to respect and play by the rules. Through fair play, we learn to win without boasting and handle disappoint with grace. Fair play also helps individuals work better with teammates and focus on the task at hand.

MATERIALS

- Labels Directions for Group Leaders (3.1)

- Labels Cards (3.2), photocopied and cut apart

- Bamboozle Cards (3.6), photocopied and cut apart

- Deck of regular playing cards

- Tape

- Writing utensils

- A Lesson 3 Exit Slip for each boy (from Appendix A)

PROCEDURE

Warm-up

- Have the boys play the Labels game according to the instructions on the Labels Directions for Group Leaders.

Activity

1. Tell the boys that today you are going to play the card game Bamboozle. Tell them that Bamboozle is played like rummy: Players attempt to get three like card values (for example, three queens, three 10s, or three aces) or three cards of the same suit in a row (for example, 9, 10, and jack of hearts.) Players are dealt seven regular playing cards to start. Each player must also draw one Bamboozle Card. (Make sure to use at least one "You must cheat" card for

every four to six players.) The player must follow the directions on the Bamboozle Card during each of his subsequent turns. Players must not disclose to other players what is on their Bamboozle Cards.

2. Play the game until you have a winner.

3. Have a discussion with the boys about fair play. Ask the boys: "What do you think *fair play* means?"

4. Have the boys show each other their Bamboozle Cards. Lead a discussion about what it was like to play a game where all players didn't adhere to the principles of fair play. Ask the boys:

   - How do you feel knowing some players were not playing fair?
   - Did you know who was cheating and who was not?
   - How did you feel if you were a player who was not playing fair?
   - Why do you think fair play is important?
   - Where might we see examples of fair play?
   - Can you think of a situation that didn't involve fair play? How did you feel?

Discussion

- What happened in Bamboozle?
- How did you feel when you knew someone was cheating?
- How did you feel if you were the one cheating?
- Ask the boys to think back to the Labels activity, then ask them the following questions:
- If someone does not play fair, is that being disrespectful?
- If someone you met didn't play fair or did not treat you with respect, how would you remember that person?
- Why is respect important?

Evaluation

STUDENT

Give each student a Lesson 3 Exit Slip to fill out, share, and hand in before leaving.

LEADER

- Did each boy participate in the activities?
- Did each boy make the connection between respect and playing fair?

Labels Directions for Group Leaders

1. Divide your group into two or more smaller groups of four to six boys. Give each group a set of labels, set facedown on the table. Have each boy stick a label to the forehead of the boy sitting next to him with a small, rolled piece of tape. Each team member may read the labels on everyone's head except his own. Members may not disclose the labels on one another's heads.

2. Give each team the task of planning a schoolwide spirit day. Tell them they will have five minutes to plan.

3. As the groups are planning, students must treat each team member according to his label.

4. After five minutes, stop the task, even if the boys are not done, and discuss the following questions:

   ▪ Were you able to plan the schoolwide spirit day? Why or why not?

   ▪ How happy are you with the results of your group?

   ▪ Were you able to guess what was on your label based on how your team members were treating you?

   ▪ How did you feel about the way you were being treated?

   ▪ Did the label a person wore result in how much respect he was shown?

From *Building Champions: A Small-Group Counseling Curriculum for Boys,* by C. Miller,
© 2016, Champaign, IL: Research Press (800-519-2707, www.researchpress.com).

Labels Cards

Leader

Helpful

Bossy

Uncooperative

Insecure

Not Interested

From *Building Champions: A Small-Group Counseling Curriculum for Boys,* by C. Miller, © 2016, Champaign, IL: Research Press (800-519-2707, www.researchpress.com).

How Do I Want to Be Remembered?

Name _____ Date _____

Below are words that describe different character traits. Circle the words that have negative meanings. Highlight the words that you would like other people to use to describe you.

Aggressive	Able	Ambitious
Annoying	Arrogant	Articulate
Bold	Bossy	Brave
Calm	Careless	Caring
Compassionate	Conceited	Confident
Creative	Curious	Dark
Deceitful	Dedicated	Defiant
Demanding	Determined	Disagreeable
Dishonest	Eager	Energetic
Forgiving	Funny	Grouchy
Hardworking	Helpful	Honest
Jealous	Joyful	Leader
Likeable	Loveable	Loyal
Miserable	Obnoxious	Organized
Outgoing	Patient	Responsible
Rude	Selfish	Serious
Shy	Silly	Smart
Strong	Stubborn	Successful
Talented	Thoughtful	Trustworthy
Untrustworthy	Vain	Vibrant
Warm	Wise	Witty

Remember Me

Name _____ Date _____

Using words from the How Do I Want to Be Remembered?
worksheet, pick 10 words that you would like other people
to use to describe you.

1. _____

2. _____

3. _____

4. _____

5. _____

6. _____

7. _____

8. _____

9. _____

10. _____

From *Building Champions: A Small-Group Counseling Curriculum for Boys,* by C. Miller,
© 2016, Champaign, IL: Research Press (800-519-2707, www.researchpress.com).

Integrity

Name _____ Date _____

With your invisible ink, write what integrity means to you.

From *Building Champions: A Small-Group Counseling Curriculum for Boys,* by C. Miller,
© 2016, Champaign, IL: Research Press (800-519-2707, www.researchpress.com).

Bamboozle Cards

Scratch your nose before each play.

Each time you draw a card, say, "Bamboozle."

You must cheat. Think of ways to hide cards and win the game.

You must cheat. Think of ways to hide cards and win the game.

Say something nice with every turn.

Each time you have cards to lay down, say, "I'm going to win!"

Cluck like a chicken if you have cards to lay down.

Make funny faces when you look at your cards.

Give someone a compliment after your turn.

Point at different items around the room to try to distract players.

If you must draw, draw two cards. Don't let anyone see you take an extra.

Before each turn, tell a player that he is doing a great job.

From *Building Champions: A Small-Group Counseling Curriculum for Boys,* by C. Miller, © 2016, Champaign, IL: Research Press (800-519-2707, www.researchpress.com).

Hands In
(Relationships)

Friendships

LEARNING OBJECTIVES

- Each boy will be able to define the word *habit*.

- Boys will be able to differentiate good friendship habits from bad friendship habits.

- Boys will understand why sometimes we may want to end certain friendships.

- Boys will understand that the way they treat others will determine the level of friendship that they will have with others.

KEY CONCEPT

A habit is a reoccurring pattern of behavior. In all aspects of our lives, we exhibit both good and bad habits. Our "relationship habits" are the ways we treat our friends. Occasionally, we must examine friendships and determine whether certain friends have bad friendship habits. Sometimes when we are in friendships where our friends treat us badly, it is okay to give ourselves permission to end the friendship.

MATERIALS

- A tennis ball, bean bag, or other small object that can be tossed between boys
- A copy for each boy:

  Friendship Habits Sorting Page (4.1)

  Friendship Habits Cards (4.2)

  Lesson 4 Exit Slip (from Appendix A)

- Whiteboard or poster board and marker
- Writing utensils
- Scissors
- Tape

PROCEDURE

Warm-up

1. Remind the boys that at the last meeting you talked about (integrity, respect, or fair play).

2. Toss the tennis ball to one boy and have him be the first to complete the statement "An example of a time I showed (integrity, respect, or fair play) was _____. " When he has responded, have him toss the tennis ball to another member to respond. Continue until everyone has answered.

3. Start again, having everyone complete the following statement: "It is important not to be known for having bad character traits because _____."

Activity

1. Have a discussion about what a habit is. Ask the boys to name some habits that they may have: biting their nails, brushing their teeth, wearing a lucky shirt, etc. Try to get the boys to list as many bad habits as good habits. List these in columns on the whiteboard or poster board.

2. Distribute the Friendship Habits Sorting Page. Ask the boys to think about habits they have with their friends and to name a few.

3. Give each boy a page of Friendship Habits Cards. Ask them to cut apart the different habits and sort into good and bad habits on their sorting page.

4. Have a discussion with the boys about each card they cut apart and sorted.

Discussion

Ask the boys:

- What can you do when a friend has bad friendship habits?

- Do you ever exhibit any bad friendship habits? Did this surprise you?

- What good friendship habits do you have that you are proud of?

- What habits do your friends have that you do not like?

- How do you feel toward a friend who has more bad friendship habits than good habits?

- If you felt a friend only had bad friendship habits, would it be okay to end the friendship? Why or why not?

- Do you think that it is normal for friendships to both form and dissolve over your lifetime? Why or why not?

Evaluation

- Give each student a Lesson 4 Exit Slip to fill out, share, and hand in before leaving.

- Did each boy participate in the activities?

- Were the boys able to identify bad friendship habits?

Trust

LEARNING OBJECTIVES

- Each boy will be able to define the word *trust*.

- Boys will understand how trust develops in a relationship.

- Boys will understand the importance of trust in different relationships.

KEY CONCEPT

Trust is the ability to have faith in another person. Trust makes relationships grow stronger. Trust exposes our vulnerabilities because we must confide in or depend on others in the hope of getting something in return. Trust requires a leap of faith, and sometimes we need to depend on others to get the job done.

MATERIALS

- A tennis ball, beanbag, or other small object that can be tossed between boys

- Blindfolds for each boy

- A piece of rope about 30 feet in length

- Writing utensils

- A copy of the Lesson 4 Exit Slip for each boy (Appendix C)

PREPARATION

Move all desks and chairs out of the way or move to a large open space like the gym or outside.

PROCEDURE

Warm-up

1. Remind the boys that at the last meeting you talked about (integrity, respect, or fair play).

2. Toss the tennis ball to one boy and have him be the first to complete this statement: "An example of a time I showed (integrity, respect, or fair play) was _____." When he has responded, have him toss the tennis ball to another member to respond.

3. Continue until everyone has answered.

4. Start again, having everyone complete the following: "It is important to not be known for having bad character traits because _____."

Activity

1. Give each participant a blindfold.

2. Explain that this is a task that will require the boys to communicate effectively with one another.

4. Position the boys in the area where the activity will take place.

5. Ask the boys to place their blindfolds over their eyes. Have the boys turn in a circle until you say stop (allow them to rotate a sufficient amount so that they become a little disoriented).

6. Make sure that the rope is coiled, then silently place it within reach of one of the boys. Explain that you have placed the rope on the floor and that on your command they must locate the rope and work together to position the rope in the shape of á perfect square on the floor.

7. Watch the boys work and make sure they are safe. Be prepared to intervene if boys wander or are at risk of bumping into furniture.

8. Allow the group 10 to 15 minutes to complete this activity. If they finish, ask them if they are satisfied with their work and then allow them to remove their blindfolds. If the group has not finished, give them a minute or two longer to complete the task. If at the end of the allotted time the group has not finished, have them remove their blindfold and process what went wrong.

9. If there is enough time, allow the group a second opportunity to complete the challenge.

Discussion

Ask the boys:

- What did we do in this activity?

- How was it to complete this task without sight?

- Who were the leaders?

- What was your confidence level at the beginning of the task?

- Were you satisfied with your results? Did you make a perfect square?

- What made this activity difficult?

- Was there a turning point that made forming the square easier?

- In what ways was trust needed for this activity?

- What did this activity teach you about trust?

- Why is trust important in relationships?

Evaluation

STUDENT

- Give each student a Lesson 4 Exit Slip to fill out, share, and hand in before leaving.

LEADER

- Did each boy participate in the activities?

- Were the boys able to talk about trust in relationships?

Values

LEARNING OBJECTIVES

- Each boy will identify the values that he deems important.

- Boys will understand that everyone has a personal set of values.

- Boys will share their values with the group.

- Boys will listen, without judgment, to the other group members.

KEY CONCEPT

Everyone has a set of values, but not everyone shares the same set of values. Our values guide our actions, and these actions can be interpreted by others who may have a value system different from ours.

MATERIALS

- A tennis ball, beanbag, or other small object that can be tossed between boys

- A copy for each boy:

  My Values (4.3)

  The Storm (4.4)

  Storm Rankings (4.5)

  Lesson 4 Exit Slip (from Appendix A)

- Writing utensils

PROCEDURE

Warm-up

1. Remind the boys that at the last meeting you talked about (integrity, respect, or fair play).

2. Toss the tennis ball to one boy and have him be the first to complete the following statement: "An example of a time I showed (integrity, respect, or fair play) was _____." When he has responded, have him toss the tennis ball to another member to respond.

3. Continue until everyone has answered.

4. Start again, having everyone complete the following: "It is important not to be known for having bad character traits because _____."

Activity

1. Distribute the My Values worksheets. Ask the boys to check the values that are important to them and discuss how every person can rank the same values in a different order. Have the boys determine the five values they deem most important.

2. Read "The Storm." Ask the boys to think about each of the story's characters.

3. Distribute the Storm Ranking worksheets and ask the boys to rate the integrity of each character in the story from 1 (most integrity) to 4 (least integrity). Encourage them to complete the sheets without discussion with the other boys.

4. When all the boys are finished, discuss how the boys ranked the story characters and why they ranked them in the order they did.

Discussion

Ask the boys:

- What were the results of this activity?

- Did everyone have the same ranking?

- Why do you think not everyone shared the same ranking? Did this surprise you?

- When someone had a ranking different from yours, do you think he had a good explanation for why he ranked the character the way he did?

- Do you think everyone here shares the same values?

- Do you think everyone here would rank the importance of each value the same?

- Why do you think people have different values?

- Do you think that we are judged on the values we have? Which values do you think most people view as desirable and undesirable?

- How do our values influence what we do at school and outside of school?

Evaluation

- Give each student a Lesson 4 Exit Slip to fill out, share, and hand in before leaving.

- Were the boys independently able to complete their worksheets?

- Did the boys listen respectfully to one another?

Friendship Habits Sorting Page

Name _____ Date _____

Good Friendship Habits

Bad Friendship Habits

From *Building Champions: A Small-Group Counseling Curriculum for Boys,* by C. Miller, © 2016, Champaign, IL: Research Press (800-519-2707, www.researchpress.com).

Friendship Habits Cards

Cut out the cards and sort them as either good friendship habits or bad friendship habits on your Friendship Habits Sorting Page. Use the blank cards to add your own friendship habits.

Puts down a friend and then says, "Only kidding!"	Constantly judges what you do.
Is a friend with someone when it's exciting to do so.	Offers advice when you need it.
Listens to his friend.	Tells other friends your secrets.
Sits with the same friends at lunch each day.	Complains about you to others.
Always has your back.	Laughs with you, not at you.
Only looks out for himself.	If the person disagrees with you, tells you and says why.

From *Building Champions: A Small-Group Counseling Curriculum for Boys,* by C. Miller, © 2016, Champaign, IL: Research Press (800-519-2707, www.researchpress.com).

My Values

Name _____ Date _____

Check the values that are important to you and rate the importance of each value you select.

☐ Family   ☐ Trustworthiness

☐ Prestige   ☐ Respect

☐ Honesty   ☐ Education

☐ Religious faith   ☐ Loyalty

☐ Power   ☐ Generosity

☐ Recognition   ☐ Health

☐ Wealth   ☐ Integrity

☐ Appearance   ☐ Work

☐ Athletic ability   ☐ Love

☐ Belonging   ☐ Friendship

☐ Teamwork   ☐ Determination

☐ Leadership   ☐ Reputation

List your top five values in order of importance.

1. _____

2. _____

3. _____

4. _____

5. _____

From *Building Champions: A Small-Group Counseling Curriculum for Boys,* by C. Miller, © 2016, Champaign, IL: Research Press (800-519-2707, www.researchpress.com).

The Storm

Name _____ Date _____

The little town of Lewisburg was devastated by a bad storm. The storm washed away many bridges and roads, and travel to and from the little town was next to impossible. Most cars and trucks encountered major water damage and were inoperable.

Jeff and Amy had been dating for over a year when the storm hit. Since the storm took the little town by surprise, many of its townspeople were not within the safety of their homes or shelter. High winds and hail caused great damage. Jeff was outside when the storm hit, and while he was running to safety, he lost his glasses.

Jeff's eyesight was very bad. Without his glasses, he could not see. Amy, who wanted to help, knew that Jeff could get another pair at the optometrist's office in the next town. Unfortunately, the bridge to the town had been washed out with the storm. There was no way to get across the river to the doctor's office for a new pair of glasses.

Amy really wanted to help. She knew her classmate, Doug, had a small boat. Amy went to Doug's house and asked if he would be willing to help her cross the river so that she could get to the next town. Doug, who could sense the desperation in Amy's voice, said that he would help her cross the river if she would pay him $1,000. Amy tried to explain to Doug that she did not have that kind of money, but he refused to make an offer Amy could afford.

Amy knew her grandmother, who lived next door to her family, kept her money hidden in her basement rather than putting it in a bank. Amy went to her grandmother's and stole the

From *Building Champions: A Small-Group Counseling Curriculum for Boys,* by C. Miller, © 2016, Champaign, IL: Research Press (800-519-2707, www.researchpress.com).

money that she needed to pay Doug to get across the river. Amy promised to herself that she would pay her grandmother back. Amy went back to Doug's house and paid him the money.

When Amy went back to Doug's, Doug took Amy's money and told her to row herself across the river. He refused to help but threatened to charge her another $1,000 if his boat was damaged or if it wasn't back before nightfall.

Amy got into the rowboat and crossed the river to the next town. She found the optometrist's office and got a replacement pair of glasses for Jeff. Excited to be able to help, Amy ran to the river and crossed back to Lewisburg.

Before going home, Amy went to Doug's house to let him know that she had returned his boat. By the time she got to Doug's house, it was beginning to get dark. When Doug opened the door and saw Amy, he told her that she owed him another $1,000. When Amy tried to reason with him, he took the glasses she got for Jeff and said that they belonged to him until he got his money. Upset, Amy left.

Amy went home and told her older brother, Harry, what happened. Harry was so mad that he went to Doug's house and got into a physical altercation. Harry took the glasses from Doug and brought them home to his sister. Amy took the glasses and ran all the way to Jeff's house.

Amy told Jeff the story about what it took to get Jeff the new glasses. Rather than being happy that he could see, Jeff was furious. He broke the glasses in half and told Amy he never wanted to see her again. He hated what she had done and said that he didn't even know who she was anymore.

Storm Rankings

Name _____ Date _____

Think about each person in the story "The Storm": Amy, Jeff, Doug, and Harry. Your job is to rank, in order, the characters with the best integrity and values to those with the least integrity and values. In addition, write the value that each character in the story exhibits in the box next to the character's name.

Rank	Character	Value
	Jeff	
	Amy	
	Doug	
	Harry	

From *Building Champions: A Small-Group Counseling Curriculum for Boys,* by C. Miller,
© 2016, Champaign, IL: Research Press (800-519-2707, www.researchpress.com).

Game Time
(Leadership and Teamwork)

Leadership

LEARNING OBJECTIVES

- Each boy will understand the concept of leadership.

- Boys will think about leadership in terms of someone who has had a positive influence on their lives.

- Boys will listen, without judgment, to the other group members.

KEY CONCEPT

Leadership is more than taking charge of a situation. Leadership can be either positive or negative depending on the impact it has on others. Effective leaders inspire others to meet goals and challenges and push them to succeed.

MATERIALS

- Wall of Leadership posters (5.1), reproduced and hung in different locations around the room

- A copy for each boy:

  Roll It (5.2)

  Lesson 5 Exit Slip (from Appendix A)

- A die

- Sticky notes

- Writing utensils

PROCEDURE

Warm-up

Distribute the Roll It worksheets to the boys. Allow each boy to roll the die; lowest number goes first. Have each boy roll the die again and answer the question associated with his roll.

Activity

1. Ask each boy to think of someone he believes is a good leader. Tell the boys not to share who they are thinking about. Give each boy three sticky notes. Ask the boys to think of three qualities that they believe the leader they are thinking of possesses. Tell them to write each quality on a separate note.

2. Now ask each boy to think of someone he believes is a bad leader. Tell the boys not to share the name of the person they are thinking about. Give each boy three more sticky notes. Ask the boys to think of three qualities that they believe the leader they are thinking of possesses. Tell them to write each quality on a separate sticky note.

3. Ask each boy to think again of the good leader and come up with some examples that make this person a good leader. Give each boy three more sticky notes. Ask the boys to write each example on separate sticky note.

4. Have the boys take their sticky notes and hang them on the appropriate posters.

5. When all the sticky notes are hung, ask the boys to take a walk around the room and read over all the responses.

6. When all the boys are finished, regroup and discuss the similarities and differences they noticed.

Discussion

Ask the boys:

- What did we do in this activity?

- Were you surprised by any answers you saw on the sticky notes?

- After seeing what others wrote, are there any additional sticky notes you would add to the posters that are hanging?

- What qualities do all (or most) of you agree are important of a good leader?

- What qualities do all (or most) of you agree are those a bad leader possesses?

- Are there examples of situations where you witnessed someone being a good leader? What did that person do to make you think he or she was a good leader?

- In what ways have you been a good leader?

- Are there situations that you can look back on and think, "I could have been a better leader?" What would you have done differently?

- What would be your leadership style?

Evaluation

- Give each student a Lesson 5 Exit Slip to fill out, share, and hand in before leaving.

- Were the boys able to see themselves as leaders?

- Were the boys able to think of areas in which they could improve their leadership skills?

Becoming a Leader

LEARNING OBJECTIVES

- Boys will define *leadership*.

- Boys will analyze characteristics of leadership.

- Boys will describe their own leadership styles.

KEY CONCEPT

Leadership can be described in various ways. Leadership can be described as the ability to move a group of people toward a goal. It is also motivating the people who follow you. Leadership involves courage and risk taking as well as knowing when to be safe. Leadership does not have a one-size-fits all definition, and everyone has their own leadership style.

MATERIALS

- Leadership posters (5.3), reproduced and hung in various locations around the room

- A copy for each boy:

  Roll It (5.2)

  Picturing Leadership (5.4)

  Lesson 5 Exit Slips (from Appendix A)

- A die

- Writing utensils

PROCEDURE

Warm-up

Distribute the Roll It worksheets to the boys. Allow each boy to roll a die; lowest number goes first. Have each boy roll the die again and answer the question associated with his roll.

Activity

1. Distribute the Picturing Leadership worksheets.

2. Ask students to take a tour around the room and view the various posters. Ask them to think about what each picture is saying about leadership. Have them write down their thoughts on the worksheet.

3. Once students have viewed all the pictures and completed their worksheets, ask them to regroup and share some of the words and phrases they have recorded.

4. After the boys have shared their thoughts about each picture, break the boys into pairs and ask them to create a definition of leadership. (Boys should mention that a leader is someone who isn't afraid to take a risk and inspires others, helps a group reach a goal, leads a team to do their best, etc.)

5. Ask groups to share their definitions with the class.

Discussion

Ask the boys:

- Explain what happened during this activity.

- When you first saw the pictures, did you think they represented leadership?

- Why do you think we looked at these pictures in relation to leadership?

- Did everyone come up with the same description of leadership for each picture? Why do you think ideas differed?

- Do any of these pictures represent any leaders you know? How?

- Which picture would describe your own leadership style? Why?

- Do you think that your definition of leadership is different after doing this activity? If so, how?

Evaluation

STUDENT

- Give each student a Lesson 5 Exit Slip to fill out, share, and hand in before leaving.

LEADER

- Were the boys able to use the pictures to generate examples of leadership?

- Were the boys able to create a definition of leadership?

OPTION 3

Teamwork

LEARNING OBJECTIVES

- Boys will identify and develop skills that are necessary for a team to be successful.

- Boys will develop communication skills among team players.

- Team members will motivate one another toward the achievement of a common goal.

KEY CONCEPT

Teamwork is as important as leadership. Teamwork is the glue that holds the team together. It is what makes the team work and reach its goal. This doesn't mean that each person will do the same thing but rather that he must work in unison with others on his own unique task. Within a team, members need to be accountable for their own actions. Failure to do so can compromise the task.

MATERIALS

- A copy for each boy:

  Roll It (5.2)

  Lesson 5 Exit Slip (from Appendix A)

- A 5 × 5–foot piece of paper or cloth

- A die

- Writing utensils

PREPARATIONS

Move furniture in the room so that the boys will have a space for their "magic carpet." Place the cloth or paper in the middle of the empty space.

PROCEDURE

Warm-up

Distribute the Roll It worksheets to the boys. Allow each boy to roll a die; lowest number goes first. Have each boy roll the die again and answer the question associated with his roll.

Activity

1. Tell the boys that the cloth or sheet of paper is a magic carpet and ask them to stand or sit on it because they will be going for a ride.

2. Once the boys are all standing or sitting on the magic carpet, tell them they have taken off and are now in the air. The problem is that right now they have no way to steer or land the magic carpet because the directions are on the bottom of the carpet.

3. Tell they boys that they must work together to turn the magic carpet over so that they can see the directions. Tell them that they may not step off the carpet and that they must turn it completely over.

Discussion

Ask the boys:

- What happened in this activity?
- When you were first asked to turn the magic carpet over, did you think this was going to be an easy or difficult task?
- How did you decide how you were going to flip the carpet over?
- Did you come up with a plan before you started, or did you just decide as you went along?
- Did a leader emerge as you worked together?
- Were some people more involved than others?
- Why was teamwork important in this activity?
- How can you relate this activity to school? To other groups or teams?

Evaluation

STUDENT

- Give each student a Lesson 5 Exit Slip to fill out, share, and hand in before leaving.

LEADER

- Did the boys all participate in the activity?
- Were the boys able to work together in a positive way?

Qualities of a Good Leader

From *Building Champions: A Small-Group Counseling Curriculum for Boys,* by C. Miller,
© 2016, Champaign, IL: Research Press (800-519-2707, www.researchpress.com).

Qualities of a Bad Leader

From *Building Champions: A Small-Group Counseling Curriculum for Boys,* by C. Miller,
© 2016, Champaign, IL: Research Press (800-519-2707, www.researchpress.com).

Roll It

Name _____ Date _____

I would define a good friendship as...

Why is trust important in a relationship?

Three things I value are...

Why do you think some friends are not good at friendship?

Trust means to me...

Is it possible to respect someone you don't trust?

From *Building Champions: A Small-Group Counseling Curriculum for Boys,* by C. Miller,
© 2016, Champaign, IL: Research Press (800-519-2707, www.researchpress.com).

From *Building Champions: A Small-Group Counseling Curriculum for Boys,* by C. Miller,
© 2016, Champaign, IL: Research Press (800-519-2707, www.researchpress.com).

From *Building Champions: A Small-Group Counseling Curriculum for Boys,* by C. Miller,
© 2016, Champaign, IL: Research Press (800-519-2707, www.researchpress.com).

From *Building Champions: A Small-Group Counseling Curriculum for Boys,* by C. Miller,
© 2016, Champaign, IL: Research Press (800-519-2707, www.researchpress.com).

From *Building Champions: A Small-Group Counseling Curriculum for Boys,* by C. Miller,
© 2016, Champaign, IL: Research Press (800-519-2707, www.researchpress.com).

From *Building Champions: A Small-Group Counseling Curriculum for Boys,* by C. Miller,
© 2016, Champaign, IL: Research Press (800-519-2707, www.researchpress.com).

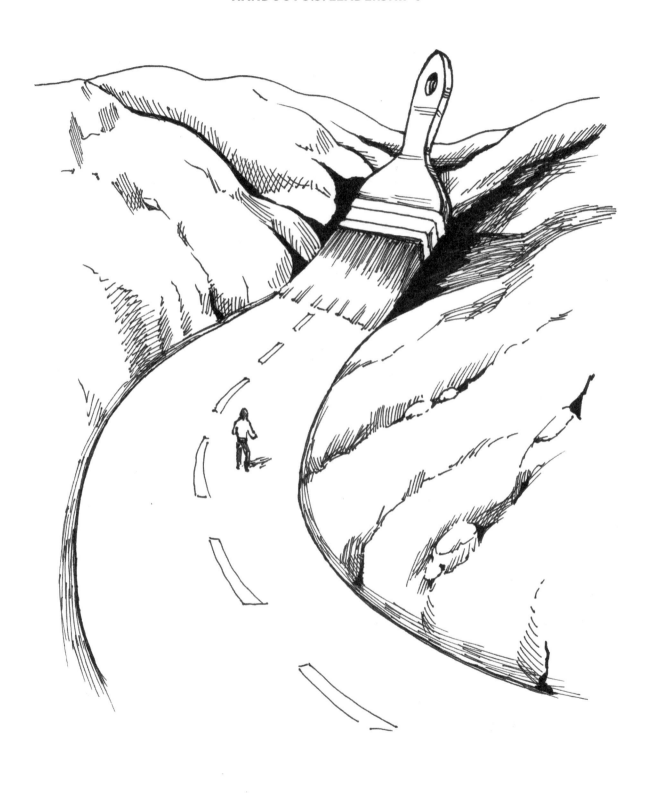

From *Building Champions: A Small-Group Counseling Curriculum for Boys,* by C. Miller,
© 2016, Champaign, IL: Research Press (800-519-2707, www.researchpress.com).

Picturing Leadership

Name _____ Date _____

Look at each picture and think about how it relates to leadership. Write down what you think the picture is saying about leadership.

Picture   **What This Picture Says About Leadership**

1   _____

        _____

2   _____

        _____

3   _____

        _____

4   _____

        _____

5   _____

        _____

6   _____

        _____

My definition of leadership:

_____

_____

_____

_____

From *Building Champions: A Small-Group Counseling Curriculum for Boys,* by C. Miller,
© 2016, Champaign, IL: Research Press (800-519-2707, www.researchpress.com).

Sitting on the Bench (Self-Control)

OPTION 1

Self-Control

LEARNING OBJECTIVES

- Boys will define self-control.

- Boys will practice self-control.

- Boys will understand the connection between self-control and developing positive personal traits.

KEY CONCEPT

Doing what is right all the time is hard to do. That is why it takes self-control to do the right thing. When we have self-control, we do and say what is right no matter how we feel or think. Without self-control, we can hurt others or ourselves without intending to do so.

MATERIALS

- Stone Face Directions for Group Leaders (6.1)

- Whiteboard or poster board and marker

- One small stone

- Writing utensils

- A copy of the Lesson 6 Exit Slip for each boy (from Appendix A)

PROCEDURE

Warm-up

1. Ask the boys to stand at the front of the room and refrain from talking. When they are all standing and quiet, ask them to line up from smallest to tallest. When they are done, ask them to line up by:

- Birthday

- Shoe size

- Number of pets they own

Check between rounds to see if they have accomplished their goal.

2. Ask the boys:

- What does this activity tell us about leadership?

- How can you relate it to what we learned last week?

- Did anyone emerge as a leader during this activity?

Activity

1. Discuss with the boys what self-control is and what it looks like. (Boys should mention staying quiet when you want to shout at someone, ignoring someone who is saying something mean to you, raising a hand in class versus blurting out an answer, etc.)

2. Using a whiteboard or poster board to record answers, brainstorm a list of problems that might result from a lack of self-control. Discuss how a lack of self-control might affect personal appearance, health, success at school, friendships, job performance, family events or relationships, etc.

3. Ask the boys to arrange the room so that one chair is at the front of the room and all others have been moved back. Section off a small space around the chair as a neutral zone.

4. Play the Stone Face game according to the directions provided.

Discussion

Ask the boys:

- Was this activity difficult?

- Were you able to maintain a stone face?

- What distracted you from keeping a straight face?

- What did this activity teach you about self-control?

- Why is self-control important?

- How can we use what we learned in this game outside school?

- Are there skills you learned in this lesson that we can use to build peace on the playground, at home, or on the bus?

Evaluation

STUDENT

- Give each student a Lesson 6 Exit Slip to fill out, share, and hand in before leaving.

- Did the boys all participate in the activity?

- Were the boys able to work together positively?

Positive Mindset

LEARNING OBJECTIVES

- Boys will learn the difference between a positive and negative mindset.

- Boys will understand that they can choose their thought patterns and focus their minds on positive thinking.

- Boys will practice changing a negative mindset into a positive mindset.

- Boys will understand the importance of looking at difficult situations from a positive mindset.

KEY CONCEPT

A positive mindset can have many benefits. Developing a positive mindset can help people cope more easily with daily life and look for solutions rather than dwelling on problems, see opportunities, believe in themselves and their abilities, and inspire and motivate others.

MATERIALS

- Whiteboard or poster board and marker

- A copy for each boy:

  Positive Mindset (6.2)

  Lesson 6 Exit Slip (from Appendix A)

- Writing utensils

PROCEDURE

Warm-up

1. Ask the boys to stand at the front of the room and to refrain from talking. When they are all standing and quiet, ask them to line up from smallest to tallest. When they are done, ask them to line up by:

   - Birthday

   - Shoe size

   - Number of pets they own

Check between rounds to see if they have accomplished their goal.

2. Ask the boys:

   - What does this activity tell us about leadership?

   - How can you relate it to what we learned last week?

   - Did anyone emerge as a leader during this activity?

Activity

1. Write "Negative Mindset" on the left side of the whiteboard or poster board and "Positive Mindset" on the right side of the board. Ask the boys to provide examples of each. For example:

   - Negative Mindset: I can't do it; It's too hard; I made a mistake; I'm stupid.

   - Positive Mindset: If I practice I will be able to do it; I'll ask for help so I can understand what is being asked; I can always improve, so I'll keep trying.

2. Discuss with the boys what it means to have a positive mindset and why it can lead to self-confidence and a healthy concept.

3. Distribute the Positive Mindset worksheets. Ask the students to change each negative thought into a Positive Mindset statement.

4. Once students have completed the worksheet, have them share their responses with the group.

Discussion

Ask the boys:

- How can changing your mindset affect your mood?

- How can having a positive mindset affect your schoolwork?

- Why is it important to look for solutions to situations that seem hopeless?

- Who are some people that have a positive mindset? How does this mindset help them?

- If you are feeling defeated, how can you remember to try to focus on a more positive mindset?

- How can you relate this to other groups or teams with which you are involved?

Evaluation

▪ Give each student a Lesson 6 Exit Slip to fill out, share, and hand in before leaving.

▪ Were the boys able to share openly with one another?

▪ Did the boys complete their worksheets?

Giving Feedback

LEARNING OBJECTIVES

- Boys will understand the importance of useful feedback.
- Boys will practice giving constructive feedback.
- Boys will accept constructive feedback from others.

KEY CONCEPT

We give and receive feedback all the time. Feedback is an important communication tool. Effective feedback can bring people together, motivate others to do a job well, and provide guidance on how to improve learning. Feedback can improve a person's confidence, self-awareness, and enthusiasm for learning.

MATERIALS

- Free Throw Directions for Group Leaders (6.3)
- A copy for each boy:

  Free Throw Group Directions (6.4)

  Lesson 6 Exit Slip (from Appendix A)
- Blindfold
- Wastepaper basket
- Four ping pong balls, soft beanbags, or balls of crumpled scrap paper
- Writing utensils

PROCEDURE

Warm-up

1. Ask the boys to stand at the front of the room and to refrain from talking. When they are all standing and quiet, ask them to line up from smallest to tallest. When they are done, ask them to line up by:

   - Birthday
   - Shoe size

■ Number of pets they own

Check between rounds to see if they have accomplished their goal.

2. Ask the boys:

   ■ What does this activity tell us about leadership?

   ■ How can you relate it to what we learned during the last lesson?

   ■ Did anyone emerge as a leader during this activity?

Activity

1. Ask the boys for a volunteer. Have the volunteer leave the room and put on a blindfold.

2. Hand out copies of the Free Throw Group Instructions to each boy.

3. Explain the directions and play the Free Throw game.

Discussion

Ask the boys:

■ What happened in this activity?

■ How did you feel about the feedback you were given during each round?

■ When is feedback useful?

■ What type of feedback is most useful?

■ How does the feedback you give assist others in being successful?

■ How can what you learned about giving and receiving feedback help you in the future?

Evaluation

STUDENT

■ Give each student a Lesson 6 Exit Slip to fill out, share, and hand in before leaving.

LEADER

■ Were the boys able to follow the instructions for the activity and give the appropriate feedback?

■ Did the boys understand the relevance of the activity to giving useful feedback?

Stone Face Directions for Group Leaders

Materials Needed

One small stone

Directions

1. Hand one group member the small stone. This boy will become the "Stone Face." The Stone Face may not move, laugh, talk, or smile. It is this person's job to refrain from showing emotion while taking on this role.

2. Have the Stone Face sit at the front of the room. Section off a neutral space (about a foot) that the other members may not cross.

3. Once the Stone Face is sitting at the front of the room, instruct the other group members to try to get the Stone Face to smile or laugh. The boys may not speak, but they may make faces or gestures to try to get the Stone Face to smile. The boys may move around the room and go up to the Stone Face, but they may not enter the neutral space around the Stone Face.

4. Allow the boys one minute to try to make the Stone Face smile or laugh. If a boy makes the Stone Face smile, then that boy becomes the Stone Face. If no one can make the Stone Face smile, then the Stone Face will choose the next Stone Face.

5. Allow each boy to have a turn being the Stone Face.

From *Building Champions: A Small-Group Counseling Curriculum for Boys,* by C. Miller, © 2016, Champaign, IL: Research Press (800-519-2707, www.researchpress.com).

Positive Mindset

Name _____ Date _____

Having a positive mindset is important to help us do our best. Look at the negative thoughts below. In the speech bubble, write what you can say to yourself to change the negative thought into a positive one.

I've practiced for weeks but I'm not good enough to make the basketball team. I'm not even going to try because everyone else is so much better than I am.

I give up!

From *Building Champions: A Small-Group Counseling Curriculum for Boys,* by C. Miller,
© 2016, Champaign, IL: Research Press (800-519-2707, www.researchpress.com).

Free Throw Directions
for Group Leaders

Materials Needed

One blindfold

Small wastepaper basket

Four ping pong balls, soft beanbags, or balls of crumpled scrap paper

Directions

1. Ask for a volunteer. Ask the volunteer to leave the room and put on the blindfold.

2. Provide the other members of the group with the Free Throw Group Instructions. Instruct the remaining students that when the volunteer reenters the room, he will have four tries to throw four balls into the wastepaper basket. The volunteer will not know where the basket is.

3. Place the wastepaper basket somewhere in the front of the room.

4. Allow the blindfolded volunteer to reenter the room. Give him the balls and ask him to try to make as many baskets as he can. You may point the volunteer in the general direction of the basket.

5. Conduct the game as follows:

   ■ Round 1: The volunteer will not know where the basket is, and during this first attempt, the other group members may not talk.

   ■ Round 2: Group members may make only negative comments ("Lousy shot," "Rubber arm," "Too bad," etc.). They may not give useful comments.

   ■ Round 3: Group members may make only positive comments ("Great job," "Keep trying," "You can do it," etc.). They may not give useful comments.

   ■ Round 4: The boys may make only useful comments ("A little to the left," "A little harder," "A little to the right," etc.).

6. When the volunteer has made his throws after each round, share with him the number of baskets he has made. Go on to the next round.

7. Repeat with another volunteer.

From *Building Champions: A Small-Group Counseling Curriculum for Boys,* by C. Miller, © 2016, Champaign, IL: Research Press (800-519-2707, www.researchpress.com).

Free Throw Group Directions

Free Throw Instructions

A volunteer will have four attempts with four shots in each attempt to make a basket. The volunteer will be blindfolded.

During each round, you may speak only as follows:

Round 1: No one talks during the volunteer's attempt to make a basket.

Round 2: Give only negative comments ("Lousy shot," "Rubber arm," "Too bad," etc.).

Round 3: Give only positive comments ("Great job," "Keep trying," "You can do it," etc.).

Round 4: Deliver only useful feedback that will help the volunteer to get the ball in ("A little to the left," "A little further," etc.).

Free Throw Instructions

A volunteer will have four attempts with four shots in each attempt to make a basket. The volunteer will be blindfolded.

During each round, you may speak only as follows:

Round 1: No one talks during the volunteer's attempt to make a basket.

Round 2: Give only negative comments ("Lousy shot," "Rubber arm," "Too bad," etc.).

Round 3: Give only positive comments ("Great job," "Keep trying," "You can do it," etc.).

Round 4: Deliver only useful feedback that will help the volunteer to get the ball in ("A little to the left," "A little further," etc.).

From *Building Champions: A Small-Group Counseling Curriculum for Boys,* by C. Miller, © 2016, Champaign, IL: Research Press (800-519-2707, www.researchpress.com).

The Last Play (Confidence)

Courage

LEARNING OBJECTIVES

- Boys will define the word *courage*.

- Boys will understand that courage requires us to make difficult choices under pressure.

- Boys will identify courage in different scenarios.

KEY CONCEPT

Courage is different from heroism. Courage is something we need when making a difficult choice about something important. In addition, courage is facing your fears and being brave. We all face difficult decisions, and sometimes we need to find the courage within to go against the crowd and stand up for what is right.

MATERIALS

- Ask, Ask, Switch Question Cards (7.1), photocopied and cut apart

- A copy for each boy:

  Courage Scenarios (7.2)

  Lesson 7 Exit Slip (from Appendix A)

- A sheet of paper

- Small book

- Writing utensils

PROCEDURE

Warm-up

1. Give each boy an Ask, Ask, Switch Question Card. Select cards from the first page of the handout that correspond to the Lesson 6 option you taught.

2. Have students pair up and play Ask, Ask, Switch. To play, have Partner 1 ask the question on his card. Partner 2 answers. Partners then switch roles: Partner 2 asks the question, and Partner 1 answers. Partners switch cards and then switch partners.

3. Continue the process until all students have partnered with someone differ- ent and have answered the questions on all cards.

Activity

1. Show the boys the sheet of paper and the book and ask, "Is there any way the paper can hold up the book if you use only one hand to hold the paper?"

2. Ask for volunteers to try. The boys will soon find this cannot be done.

3. Take the paper and roll it tightly into a one-inch diameter tube. Hold the tube in one hand and carefully place the book on top of the open end of the tube. It should support the book.

4. Relate this illustration to the ability we all have to turn our weaknesses into strengths and show courage. Point out that the unrolled paper was flimsy and weak and was crushed by the book. Continue explaining that the rolled paper tube became stronger and was able to hold up under pressure. Explain that in times of pressure we have choices to make.

5. Ask the boys:

    ■ How can the unrolled paper be compared to a person faced with a diffi- cult decision?

    ■ What does the rolled paper represent?

    ■ Are there times when we feel under pressure and we could choose either to be flimsy like the unrolled paper or strong like the paper tube?

    ■ Does anyone have an example of a situation where either you or someone you know had to choose to be weak or strong?

    ■ What are some ways we can turn weaknesses into strengths?

6. Hand out the Courage Scenarios worksheet. Have the boys read a scenario and discuss as a group. Determine as a group whether each scenario required courage.

Discussion

Ask the boys:

■ What happened in this activity?

■ What does courage mean to you?

■ What are some ways that you can show courage?

■ How is courage different from being a hero?

■ Do people gain courage when they face something horrible?

- What are ways you can be courageous?

Evaluation

STUDENT

- Give each student a Lesson 7 Exit Slip to fill out, share, and hand in before leaving.

LEADER

- Were the boys able to make a connection between courage and being able to stay strong under pressure?

- Did the boys share examples of times they showed courage?

Responsibility

LEARNING OBJECTIVES

- Boys will learn what it means to be responsible.

- Boys will learn to make responsible choices.

- Boys will understand that taking responsibility means accepting consequences for their behaviors.

KEY CONCEPT

Being responsible means being accountable for one's own actions. People who are responsible accept the consequences of their actions and behaviors without making excuses or blaming others. When we accept responsibility for our actions, we are trusted by others. In addition, when we act irresponsibly we can put others in harm's way.

MATERIALS

- Ask, Ask, Switch Question Cards (7.1), photocopied and cut apart

- A copy for each boy:

  Brainstorming Responsibility (7.3)

  Importance of Responsibility (7.4)

  Lesson 7 Exit Slip (from Appendix A)

- Writing utensils

PROCEDURE

Warm-up

1. Give each boy an Ask, Ask, Switch Question Card. Select cards from the first page of the handout that correspond to the Lesson 6 option you taught.

2. Have students pair up and play Ask, Ask, Switch. To play, have Partner 1 ask the question on his card. Partner 2 answers. Partners then switch roles: Partner 2 asks the question, and Partner 1 answers. Partners switch cards and then switch partners.

3. Continue the process until all students have partnered with someone different and have answered the questions on all cards.

Activity

1. Separate the boys into four groups. Tell them that today they will discuss what it means to be responsible.

2. Distribute the Brainstorming Responsibility worksheets and assign each group a question to discuss:

   ■ Group 1: What does it mean to be responsible?

   ■ Group 2: What are some responsibilities boys your age have?

   ■ Group 3: Think of some adults you know. What are the different responsibilities they each have?

   ■ Group 4: What are consequences we face for being irresponsible?

3. Allow groups to brainstorm responses to their question. After several minutes, bring the groups back together and have the smaller groups discuss their ideas with the entire group.

4. Distribute the Importance of Responsibility worksheets. Allow time for the boys to complete their worksheets and discuss as a group.

Discussion

Ask the boys:

■ Why is it important to be responsible?

■ How does being responsible help us to earn other people's trust?

■ What do you think of someone who isn't being responsible and tries to blame his or her lack of responsibility on someone else?

■ What are the do's and don'ts of responsibility?

■ How would our world be different if we all always took responsibility for our actions?

Evaluation

STUDENT

■ Give each student a Lesson 7 Exit Slip to fill out, share, and hand in before leaving.

- Did the boys understand what it means to be responsible?

- Did the boys make a connection between being responsible and accepting the consequences of their behaviors and actions?

Balance

LEARNING OBJECTIVES

- Boys will demonstrate the ability to balance school, homework, extracurricular activities, family, and friendships to lead a healthy lifestyle.

- Boys will recognize the importance of having a variety of interests and abilities.

- Boys will understand how balance is an important component of a healthy lifestyle.

KEY CONCEPT

We all need to find balance in our lives in terms of family, friends, work, health, etc. It can be tough to balance homework, chores, friends, family, sports and activities, and fun. Sometimes it can feel like a huge juggling act. Finding balance is important for a healthy lifestyle.

MATERIALS

- Ask, Ask, Switch Question Cards (7.1), photocopied and cut apart

- A copy for each boy:

  What Are Your Spokes? (7.5)

  Lesson 7 Exit Slip (from Appendix A)

- Whiteboard or poster board and marker

- Writing utensils

PROCEDURE

Warm-up

1. Give each boy an Ask, Ask, Switch Question Card. Select cards from the first page of the handout that correspond to the Lesson 6 option you taught.

2. Have students pair up and play Ask, Ask, Switch. To play, have Partner 1 ask the question on his card. Partner 2 answers. Partners then switch roles: Partner 2 asks the question, and Partner 1 answers. Partners switch cards and then switch partners.

3. Continue the process until all students have partnered with someone different and have answered the questions on all cards.

Activity

1. Discuss with the boys the idea of having a balanced life. A balanced life means balancing all those things that are important to you: your activities, your sports, your family, homework, school, friends, and so forth while still taking care of yourself and the people who are important to you. A well-balanced person has the ability to focus his attention and energy on attaining his goals, is less stressed, and tends to be positive and happy.

2. On the whiteboard or poster board, label three columns "Things I Have to Do," "Commitments," and "Goals." Ask the boys to think about their lives and ask them to list aspects that would fall under each category.

3. Hand out the What Are Your Spokes? worksheets and ask boys to think about balance and what they have listed on the board. Some examples might be the following:

   - Hockey player—sports

   - Going to the mall with friends—friendship

   - Great at math—school

   - Like to laugh—emotional

   - Playing video games—friends

   - Going to church every Sunday—family

4. Have the boys complete their worksheets and then discuss as a group.

Discussion

Ask the boys:

- Why did we use spokes to represent activities that are important to us?

- Which part of your wheel had the most spokes?

- What happens to a wheel that has few spokes? Would the wheel hold up to pressure?

- What happens if we focus our lives on just one activity or idea? Are we more susceptible to stress and burnout?

- Do you have a balanced approach to your life?

- Does the wheel show that you are focused too heavily on any one area of your life? Are there any areas where you are focused too lightly?

- Do you struggle to find balance?

- What can you do to help yourself have balance in your life?

Evaluation

- Give each student a Lesson 7 Exit Slip to fill out, share, and hand in before leaving.

- Were the boys able to identify a variety of spokes on their wheel?

- Did the boys understand the connection between the numbers of spokes on the wheel relative to balance?

Ask, Ask, Switch Question Cards

Q What is self-control?

Lesson 6: Option 1

Q Why is it important to practice self-control?

Lesson 6: Option 1

Q What is a positive mindset?

Lesson 6: Option 2

Q Why is important to have a positive mindset?

Lesson 6: Option 2

Q What is feedback?

Lesson 6: Option 3

Q How can giving feedback be a useful tool?

Lesson 6: Option 3

From *Building Champions: A Small-Group Counseling Curriculum for Boys,* by C. Miller,
© 2016, Champaign, IL: Research Press (800-519-2707, www.researchpress.com).

(Handout 7.1, continued)

Q What do teammates need to do in order to work well as a team?

Q What personal qualities are important in friendships?

Q What is a current goal you have for yourself?

Q What are qualities you want to be recognized for?

Q What have you learned about leadership?

Q Why is goal setting important?

Q What has been your favorite activity in Building Champions?

Q What is one thing you have learned in Building Champions?

Courage Scenarios

Name _____ Date _____

***Read over each situation and determine if it is or is not
an example of courage.***

1. You saw your friend take money out of someone else's back-pack in the locker room during PE class. He told you he'd split the money with you if you didn't tell. After PE was over, the person whose locker it was noticed the money was missing. Now your PE teacher is confronting your class, trying to find out who took the money. You decide to tell the PE teacher who took the money when nobody else is around.

2. Your dog is very old and very sick. The vet tells you and your parents he must be put down. You ask for a few minutes with your dog to say goodbye.

3. You were told that you wouldn't be able to go to Jack's birthday party if you didn't keep your room clean for the week.

4. All your friends are going to sleepaway camp. Your parents said that you could go as well, but you've never been away from home before and are afraid to be away for so long.

5. Caden knows he has a lot of homework, but he doesn't know how he will get it all done and go to baseball practice.

6. You are new to a school and haven't made any friends yet. You try out for the football team, even though you have never played before and worry that you won't be good enough.

7. Doug's friends are going over to Nick's house to watch a horror movie marathon. You get nightmares every time you see scary movies, but you don't want to miss out on a night of hanging out with your friends. You decide to go to Nick's.

From *Building Champions: A Small-Group Counseling Curriculum for Boys,* by C. Miller,
© 2016, Champaign, IL: Research Press (800-519-2707, www.researchpress.com).

Brainstorming Responsibility

Brainstorming Responsibility: Group 1

Brainstorm with your group an answer to the following question:

What does it mean to be responsible?

Brainstorming Responsibility: Group 2

Brainstorm with your group an answer to the following question:

What are some responsibilities boys your age have?

From *Building Champions: A Small-Group Counseling Curriculum for Boys,* by C. Miller,
© 2016, Champaign, IL: Research Press (800-519-2707, www.researchpress.com).

(Handout 7.3, continued)

Brainstorming Responsibility: Group 3

Brainstorm with your group an answer to the following question:

Think of some adults you know. What are the different responsibilities they each have?

Brainstorming Responsibility: Group 4

Brainstorm with your group an answer to the following question:

What are consequences we face for being irresponsible?

From *Building Champions: A Small-Group Counseling Curriculum for Boys,* by C. Miller,
© 2016, Champaign, IL: Research Press (800-519-2707, www.researchpress.com).

Importance of Responsibility

Name _____ Date _____

Think about each career. List the different job responsibilities of each career and then the consequences if someone in that career acted irresponsibly. What would happen?

Career	Job Responsibilities	Consequences of Irresponsibility
Police officer		
Teacher		
Accountant		
Car mechanic		
Physician		

From *Building Champions: A Small-Group Counseling Curriculum for Boys,* by C. Miller,
© 2016, Champaign, IL: Research Press (800-519-2707, www.researchpress.com).

What Are Your Spokes?

Name_____ Date_____

Spokes on a bicycle help to keep the wheel in balance. The more spokes there are, the more support the wheel has.

- Draw and label as many spokes as apply to you on the wheel. Make sure to include everything that is important to you and keeps your life in balance (sports, family, friends, school, clubs).

- Once you have completed your wheel, darken the spokes that are most important to you.

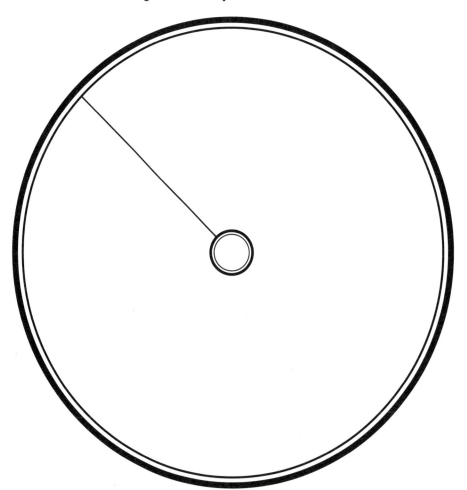

From *Building Champions: A Small-Group Counseling Curriculum for Boys,* by C. Miller,
© 2016, Champaign, IL: Research Press (800-519-2707, www.researchpress.com).

Shake Hands, Game Over
(Being a Good Sport)

Being a Good Sport

LEARNING OBJECTIVES

- Boys will practice being a good sport.

- Boys will gain knowledge of the basic principles of being a good sport.

- Boys will understand the importance of being a good sport in everyday life.

KEY CONCEPT

We all know the saying "It's not whether you win or lose, but how you play the game." Being a good sport is important in both competition and in our daily lives. Playing fair, showing respect, and being responsible for ourselves builds champions both on and off the court.

MATERIALS

- Two Cents Directions for Group Leaders (8.1)

- Two Cents graphic (8.2), copied and cut apart so every boy has two pennies

- A copy for each boy:

  Building Champions Pre-Group/Post-Group Survey (from Appendix C)

  Certificate of Completion (8.2)

- Yardstick or other long, thin, straight stick

- Writing utensils

- Celebratory treat of choice

PROCEDURE

Warm-up

Have the boys sit in a circle. Give each boy two pennies, cut from the graphic. Play the game according to the Two Cents Directions for Group Leaders.

Activity

1. Give out celebratory treats to the boys.

2. Ask the boys if they have ever heard the saying "It's not whether you win or lose, it's how you play the game." Have them explain what the saying means. Ask them:

   ▪ What does this quote mean in terms of being a good sport?

   ▪ How would you describe being a good sport?

3. Tell the boys that they will be practicing being a good sport by working together to lower a "helium stick" from their shoulders to their knees.

4. Ask the boys to line up in two rows facing each other and introduce the helium stick (the yardstick). Conduct the activity as follows:

   ▪ Ask the boys to point their index fingers and hold their arms out just below their chins.

   ▪ Lay the helium stick down on the boys' fingers. Get the boys to adjust their finger heights until the helium stick is horizontal and everyone's index fingers are touching the stick.

   ▪ Challenge the boys to lower the helium stick to the ground. Each person's fingers must be in contact with the stick at all times. If anyone's finger isn't touching the stick, the challenge should be restarted.

5. Ask the boys:

   ▪ What happened in this activity?

   ▪ Before I handed you the helium stick, did you think this was going to be easy or difficult? What did you think when you first started?

   ▪ How did you do in being a good sport as you tried to lower the stick?

   ▪ How can you relate what you have learned about being a good sport to school?

6. Have the boys complete the Building Champions Pre-Group/Post-Group Survey.

7. Award each boy a Building Champions Certificate of Completion.

8. Thank the boys for participating in group, ask them to all put their hands in a circle, and end group with a team cheer (e.g., "Yay, group!").

Two Cents Directions for Group Leaders

1. Before the boys come to group, photocopy and cut out the pennies from the Two Cents graphic so that each boy has a total of two cents. (You may use real pennies for this activity if you prefer.)

2. When the boys come to Building Champions, have them sit in a circle.

3. Introduce the warm-up by commenting about how throughout the year everyone has contributed their "two cents." Continue to say how normally when someone shares their two cents it usually refers to their trying to benefit the group by providing their ideas.

4. Give every boy two pennies and tell the boys that they are to give away their two cents to other individuals in the group. The only stipulation is that to give away a penny, the boy must identify a positive quality that he has admired about the individual to whom he is giving a penny. The goal is for the boys to try to give away all their pennies, even the ones they receive.

5. After the activity, discuss the following questions:

    ■ How difficult was it to give away all your pennies?

    ■ What did group members most appreciate about you?

    ■ How did it feel to receive compliments from group members?

    ■ How did it feel to give a compliment to others?

From *Building Champions: A Small-Group Counseling Curriculum for Boys,* by C. Miller,
© 2016, Champaign, IL: Research Press (800-519-2707, www.researchpress.com). **141**

Two Cents

From *Building Champions: A Small-Group Counseling Curriculum for Boys,* by C. Miller,
© 2016, Champaign, IL: Research Press (800-519-2707, www.researchpress.com).

Certificate of Completion

This certificate is awarded to

_____

Congratulations on your completion of the

Building Champions Program.

You have developed many new skills and are ready to be a leader and role model to others!

_____   _____
Group leader   Date

From *Building Champions: A Small-Group Counseling Curriculum for Boys,* by C. Miller,
© 2016, Champaign, IL: Research Press (800-519-2707, www.researchpress.com).

Exit Slips

Building Champions   **Lesson 1 Exit Slip**

1. One thing that excites me about this group is:

   _____

   _____

2. Being a champion means to me:

   _____

   _____

Building Champions   **Lesson 1 Exit Slip**

1. One thing that excites me about this group is:

   _____

   _____

2. Being a champion means to me:

   _____

   _____

Building Champions   **Lesson 1 Exit Slip**

1. One thing that excites me about this group is:

   _____

   _____

2. Being a champion means to me:

   _____

   _____

From *Building Champions: A Small-Group Counseling Curriculum for Boys,* by C. Miller,
© 2016, Champaign, IL: Research Press (800-519-2707, www.researchpress.com).

Building Champions   **Lesson 2 Exit Slip**

1. One way I can be accountable for myself is:

   _____

   _____

2. One thing I learned about myself today was:

   _____

   _____

- -

Building Champions   **Lesson 2 Exit Slip**

1. One way I can be accountable for myself is:

   _____

   _____

2. One thing I learned about myself today was:

   _____

   _____

- -

Building Champions   **Lesson 2 Exit Slip**

1. One way I can be accountable for myself is:

   _____

   _____

2. One thing I learned about myself today was:

   _____

   _____

From *Building Champions: A Small-Group Counseling Curriculum for Boys,* by C. Miller,
© 2016, Champaign, IL: Research Press (800-519-2707, www.researchpress.com).

Building Champions **Lesson 3 Exit Slip**

1. I want to be remembered for these qualities:

    _____

    _____

2. One thing I learned about myself today was:

    _____

    _____

- -

Building Champions **Lesson 3 Exit Slip**

1. I want to be remembered for these qualities:

    _____

    _____

2. One thing I learned about myself today was:

    _____

    _____

- -

Building Champions **Lesson 3 Exit Slip**

1. I want to be remembered for these qualities:

    _____

    _____

2. One thing I learned about myself today was:

    _____

    _____

From *Building Champions: A Small-Group Counseling Curriculum for Boys,* by C. Miller,
© 2016, Champaign, IL: Research Press (800-519-2707, www.researchpress.com).

Building Champions   **Lesson 4 Exit Slip**

1. One thing I learned that surprised me today was:

   _____

   _____

2. A good friend is:

   _____

   _____

Building Champions   **Lesson 4 Exit Slip**

1. One thing I learned that surprised me today was:

   _____

   _____

2. A good friend is:

   _____

   _____

Building Champions   **Lesson 4 Exit Slip**

1. One thing I learned that surprised me today was:

   _____

   _____

2. A good friend is:

   _____

   _____

From *Building Champions: A Small-Group Counseling Curriculum for Boys,* by C. Miller,
© 2016, Champaign, IL: Research Press (800-519-2707, www.researchpress.com).

Building Champions **Lesson 5 Exit Slip**

1. Leadership is:

   _____

   _____

2. One thing that surprised me today was:

   _____

   _____

Building Champions **Lesson 5 Exit Slip**

1. Leadership is:

   _____

   _____

2. One thing that surprised me today was:

   _____

   _____

Building Champions **Lesson 5 Exit Slip**

1. Leadership is:

   _____

   _____

2. One thing that surprised me today was:

   _____

   _____

From *Building Champions: A Small-Group Counseling Curriculum for Boys,* by C. Miller,
© 2016, Champaign, IL: Research Press (800-519-2707, www.researchpress.com).

Building Champions **Lesson 6 Exit Slip**

1. I can use what I learned today by:

   _____

   _____

2. My favorite part of group today was:

   _____

   _____

Building Champions **Lesson 6 Exit Slip**

1. I can use what I learned today by:

   _____

   _____

2. My favorite part of group today was:

   _____

   _____

Building Champions **Lesson 6 Exit Slip**

1. I can use what I learned today by:

   _____

   _____

2. My favorite part of group today was:

   _____

   _____

From *Building Champions: A Small-Group Counseling Curriculum for Boys,* by C. Miller,
© 2016, Champaign, IL: Research Press (800-519-2707, www.researchpress.com).

Building Champions

1. How do choices I make affect my life?

_____

_____

2. The biggest lesson I learned today was:

_____

_____

Building Champions

1. How do choices I make affect my life?

_____

_____

2. The biggest lesson I learned today was:

_____

_____

Building Champions

1. How do choices I make affect my life?

_____

_____

2. The biggest lesson I learned today was:

_____

_____

From *Building Champions: A Small-Group Counseling Curriculum for Boys,* by C. Miller,
© 2016, Champaign, IL: Research Press (800-519-2707, www.researchpress.com).

Program Organization and Progress Tracking Forms

Building Champions Small-Group Action Plan

Goal: To help upper elementary through middle school boys build trust, respect and peer connections while reducing classroom conflicts, discipline issues, and anxiety.

Target Group: # of students _____ grade(s) _____

Data Used to Identify Students: _____

School Counselor	ASCA Domain, Standard and Student Competency	Outline of Group Sessions to Be Delivered	Resources Needed	Process Data (Number of students affected)	Perception Data (types of surveys used)	Outcome Data (achievement, attendance and/or behavior data collected)	Project Start/ Project End
		Week 1 – Introduction Week 2 – Breaking a Sweat Week 3 – In the Huddle Week 4 – Hands In Week 5 – Game Time Week 6 – Sitting on the Bench Week 7 – The Last Play Week 8 – Shake Hands	Building Champions curriculum, playground ball, cards, paper, tape, markers/ craft supplies, beanbags, writing utensils, pennies, index cards, dice, blindfolds, bow, whistle, clay, straws, highlighers, lemon juice, paintbrush, iron, towel, cereal box, rope, sticky notes, stone, small book, yardstick		Teacher referral form, parent survey pre- and post-survey, student follow-up form, weekly exit slips	Achievement Behavior Attendance	

From *Building Champions: A Small-Group Counseling Curriculum for Boys*, by C. Miller,
© 2016, Champaign, IL: Research Press (800-519-2707, www.researchpress.com).

Building Champions Teacher Referral Form

I am starting a small group for boys called Building Champions that will be offered during _____ [name scheduled time(s)]. The group's goal is to foster trust, respect, and peer connections while reducing classroom conflicts, discipline issues, and anxiety. The group will meet once a week for eight weeks and will provide students with an opportunity to engage with fellow classmates on a more personal level. Students will participate in a variety of activities and projects while focusing on a daily themed lesson.

I am seeking your input for students that might benefit from this program. Please use the form below to refer any of your students to the Building Champions group.

Teacher name _____

Student name	Grade	Discipline	Peer relations	Anxiety	Other Notes

Please return by _____ to _____.

From *Building Champions: A Small-Group Counseling Curriculum for Boys*, by C. Miller,
© 2016, Champaign, IL: Research Press (800-519-2707, www.researchpress.com).

Building Champions Parent/Guardian Consent Form

Dear Parent and/or Guardian of _____:

I am starting a small group called Building Champions that will be offered once a week for the next eight weeks. The group's goal is to foster trust, respect, and peer connections while reducing classroom conflicts, discipline issues, and anxiety. The group provides boys with an opportunity to meet with fellow classmates on a more personal level. Students will participate in a variety of activities and projects while focusing on a daily themed lesson. The overall goal is for boys to learn that they are in control of their attitudes, behaviors, and success and to come to understand that with perseverance they can be champions at life.

I would like your son to be a member of this group. Attached is a permission slip, which needs to be signed and returned in order for your son to participate. Please feel free to contact me at _____ if you have any questions.

Sincerely,

School Counselor

I give permission for my child, _____, to participate in the Building Champions program.

_____   _____
Parent/guardian   Date

From *Building Champions: A Small-Group Counseling Curriculum for Boys,* by C. Miller,
© 2016, Champaign, IL: Research Press (800-519-2707, www.researchpress.com).

Building Champions Attendance Tracker

Name	Lesson 1 Topic—Introduction	Lesson 2 Topic— Breaking a Sweat	Lesson 3 Topic— In the Huddle	Lesson 4 Topic—Hands In

From *Building Champions: A Small-Group Counseling Curriculum for Boys,* by C. Miller,
© 2016, Champaign, IL: Research Press (800-519-2707, www.researchpress.com).

(*Building Champions Attendance Tracker, continued*)

Name	Lesson 5 Topic—Game Time	Lesson 6 Topic—Sitting on the Bench	Lesson 7 Topic—The Last Play	Lesson 8 Topic—Shake Hands, Game Over

From *Building Champions: A Small-Group Counseling Curriculum for Boys*, by C. Miller,
© 2016, Champaign, IL: Research Press (800-519-2707, www.researchpress.com).

Building Champions Data Tracker

Use this form to record data and analyze the impact of your group.

Student name	Pregroup			Postgroup	
	Does student use appropriate coping skills?	Has student exhibited behavior problems?	Has student had academic performance problems?	Does student use appropriate coping skills?	Has student behavior improved?	Has student's academic performance improved?

From *Building Champions: A Small-Group Counseling Curriculum for Boys*, by C. Miller, © 2016, Champaign, IL: Research Press (800-519-2707, www.researchpress.com).

Building Champions Lesson Planner

Lesson	Date	Lesson	Concept covered	Materials needed
1				
2				
3				
4				
5				
6				
7				
8				

From *Building Champions: A Small-Group Counseling Curriculum for Boys,* by C. Miller,
© 2016, Champaign, IL: Research Press (800-519-2707, www.researchpress.com).

Program Evaluation Forms

Building Champions Pre-Group/Post-Group Survey

Name_____Date_____

Please check the response that you feel best describes you.

1. In school I feel like I am part of a team.

   ❏ Yes   ❏ No

2. When I disagree with my friend, I can voice my opinion without arguing.

   ❏ Yes   ❏ No

3. When I fight with my friends, I feel in control of my emotions.

   ❏ Yes   ❏ No

4. I experience anxiety at school.

   ❏ Often   ❏ Sometimes   ❏ Never

5. I can have a positive impact on my school.

   ❏ Yes   ❏ No

6. I would describe myself as a champion.

   ❏ Yes   ❏ No

7. Being a champion means to me:

   _____

   _____

8. Three qualities of a champion include:

   a. _____

   b. _____

   c. _____

9. I solve conflicts by:

   _____

   _____

10. I am a leader because:

   _____

   _____

From *Building Champions: A Small-Group Counseling Curriculum for Boys,* by C. Miller,
© 2016, Champaign, IL: Research Press (800-519-2707, www.researchpress.com).

Building Champions Group Member Program Evaluation

Name _____ Date _____

Please check the response that you feel best describes you.

1. I enjoyed my time in Building Champions.

   ❏ Yes   ❏ No

2. My leader was helpful.

   ❏ Yes   ❏ No

3. I felt comfortable expressing my ideas and opinions in Building Champions.

   ❏ Yes   ❏ No

4. One thing I learned in group was:

   _____

   _____

5. Is there anything I would change in Building Champions?

   ❏ Yes   ❏ No

   If "yes," I would change: _____

   _____

   _____

6. I would recommend Building Champions to a friend.

   ❏ Yes   ❏ No

From *Building Champions: A Small-Group Counseling Curriculum for Boys,* by C. Miller,
© 2016, Champaign, IL: Research Press (800-519-2707, www.researchpress.com).

Building Champions Parent/Guardian Follow-up Letter

Dear Parent or Guardian of _____:

Thank you for allowing your son to be a part of our Building Champions program these last few weeks. Your son has learned many new skills and has himself become a champion.

We covered the following topics:

- Lesson 1: Introduction to Building Champions (What Is a Champion?)

- Lesson 2: Breaking a Sweat (Goal Setting)

- Lesson 3: In the Huddle (Integrity and Respect)

- Lesson 4: Hands In (Relationships)

- Lesson 5: Game Time (Leadership and Teamwork)

- Lesson 6: Sitting on the Bench (Self-Control)

- Lesson 7: The Last Play (Confidence)

- Lesson 8: Shake Hands, Game Over (Being a Good Sport)

I would appreciate input from you about your child's experience in the small group. Please complete the attached Building Champions program evaluation and send the completed form back to school with your child by _____.

Thank you for your support and feedback. Please contact me if you have questions or concerns.

Sincerely,

Group Leader

Building Champions Parent/Guardian Program Evaluation

This is a survey about changes your son has made at home while participating in the group at school and since the group ended. The survey will help us meet the needs of ALL students more effectively. The survey is anonymous unless you want the group leader to contact you. Thank you for taking the time to complete this form. Your feedback is important.

Before the group started, I hoped my child would learn:

I've noticed these changes in my child's behavior and/or attitude as a result of participating in the group:

Please circle your opinion about the following:

1. My son benefited from the Building Champions group.	Highly agree	Somewhat agree	Do not agree
2. My son enjoyed working with the other boys in the group.	Highly agree	Somewhat agree	Do not agree
3. My son enjoyed working with the leader in the group.	Highly agree	Somewhat agree	Do not agree
4. My son has better control over his emotions.	Highly agree	Somewhat agree	Do not agree
5. I would recommend Building Champions to other families.	Highly agree	Somewhat agree	Do not agree

The following information is optional:

_____   _____
Parent/guardian name   Contact phone or email

From *Building Champions: A Small-Group Counseling Curriculum for Boys,* by C. Miller, © 2016, Champaign, IL: Research Press (800-519-2707, www.researchpress.com).

Building Champions Teacher Program Evaluation

Our boys' group, Building Champions, has been completed. The group's goal has been to foster friendships, encourage positive peer relations, and develop leadership skills. I am seeking your evaluation of a student who has participated in this program. Please complete this form to let me know if the Building Champions group has had a positive impact on the boy involved.

Student name _____ Teacher name _____

1. Did the student's grades change over the course of the Building Champions program? If so, what was the change?

2. Has the student had fewer discipline issues since the start of the program?

3. Is the student exhibiting more positive relationships with his peers?

4. Is there any other information that you would like to share about the impact of Building Champions program?

Please return by _____ to _____.

From *Building Champions: A Small-Group Counseling Curriculum for Boys,* by C. Miller,
© 2016, Champaign, IL: Research Press (800-519-2707, www.researchpress.com).

Building Champions Group Member Follow-up

It's been a month since our group, Building Champions, has ended. I am interested in knowing how you are doing since the group ended. Please let me know how things are going. I can't wait to hear from you!

Name _____ Date _____

1. What do you remember from the group?

2. Since Building Champions ended, are you better able to control your emotions when you are in a difficult or frustrating situation?

3. Are relationships with your friends better?

4. Are you still friends with the boys from group?

5. Is there any other information that you would like to share about the Building Champions program?

Please return by _____ to _____.

From *Building Champions: A Small-Group Counseling Curriculum for Boys,* by C. Miller,
© 2016, Champaign, IL: Research Press (800-519-2707, www.researchpress.com).

REFERENCES

American School Counselor Association. (2012). *The ASCA National Model: A Framework for School Counseling Programs* (3rd ed.). Alexandria, VA: Author.

American School Counselor Association. (2014). *Mindsets and behaviors for student success: K–12 college- and career-readiness standards for every student.* Alexandria, VA: Author.

Downey, D. B., & Vogt Yuan, A. S. (2005). Sex differences in school performance during high school: Puzzling patterns and possible explanations. *The Sociological Quarterly, 46,* 299–321.

Hall, G., & Charmaraman, L. (2011). Growing boys: Implementing a boys' empowerment group in an afterschool program. *Afterschool Matters, 13,* 49–51.

Jackson, T. (1993). *Activities that teach.* Sedona, AZ: Red Rock Publishing.

Mid-Atlantic Equity Consortium. (2010). *Adolescent boys: Statistics and trends.* Retrieved May 11, 2015, from http://files.eric.ed.gov/fulltext/EJ980179.pdf

Thompson, M. (n.d.). *Understanding and raising boys: Boys in school.* Retrieved May 12, 2015, from http://www.pbs.org/parents/raisingboys/school.html

U. S. Department of Education, Office of Civil Rights. (2012). *Gender equity in education.* Retrieved May 12, 2015, from http://www2.ed.gov/about/offices/list/ocr/docs/gender-equity-in-education.pdf

OVERTIME: ADDITIONAL RESOURCES

Here are some additional resources to help your game in case your Building Champions group runs into extra innings.

Websites

- The Ophelia Project: http://www.opheliaproject.org
- Kids Empowered: http://kidsempowered.com
- Boys to Men Mentoring: http://boystomen.org
- Stop Bullying Now: http://www.stopbullying.gov
- Teaching Tolerance: http://www.tolerance.org

Publications

Balducci, R. (2010). *How do you tuck in a superhero? and other delightful mysteries of raising boys.* Grand Rapids, MI: Revell.

Biddulph, S. (2014). *Raising boys: Why boys are different—and how to help them become happy and well-balanced men* (3rd ed.). New York: Ten Speed Press.

James, S., & Thomas, D. (2009). *Wild things: The art of nurturing boys.* Carol Stream, IL: Tyndale House.

Wiseman, R. (2014). *Masterminds and wingmen: Helping our boys cope with schoolyard power, locker-room tests, girlfriends, and the new rules of the Boy World.* New York: Harmony.

ABOUT THE AUTHOR

Carol Miller is a certified school counselor for the Lansing Central School District in Lansing, New York, and has worked as a school counselor for over 20 years. She received her bachelor's degree in anthropology at the State University of New York at Albany before pursuing her master's degree in school guidance and counseling from Sage Graduate School in Troy, New York. Carol has experience as an elementary, high school, and middle school counselor. She is the founder and author of the Middle School Counselor blog (www.themiddleschoolcounselor.com) and the founder of several popular Facebook school counselor groups.

Carol won the 2014 New York State Counselor of the Year Award for her dedication to her students and the counseling profession. She has presented nationally for the American School Counselor Association (ASCA), New York State School Counselor Association (NYSSCA), and the National Conference on Girl Bullying. She is a vice president of middle level school counseling for NYSSCA and a member and past president of the Tompkins Area Counselor Association, and she holds membership in ASCA, the National Association for College Admission Counseling, and the New York State Association for College Admission Counseling.

In her free time, Carol is a crafter at heart, a youth soccer and basketball coach, and a hockey mom to her three sons.